BE EMPOWERED™: A TO Z

Your Guide to Living Life Unlimited

Asiah Wolfolk-Manning, Esq.

Acknowledgements

My motto is "The only way I fail is if I choose not to succeed." I have been blessed to be successful in many endeavors because the people around me have been encouraging and supportive. To my husband, Rod, thank you for allowing me the time and space to pursue my purpose and passion in life. Thank you for always believing in me and being my partner in life.

A special thanks to my editor, Neca C. Smith. You were a great help to me when I needed it most. To my great-grandmother, Thelma Battle, thank you for teaching me to believe dreams can come true and empowering me to become the woman I was created to be.

To Tristan, I am forever grateful I was chosen to be your mom. I want you to know there is no limit to what you can accomplish in life because you have unlimited talent, unlimited opportunities, and unlimited potential. The world is waiting for you to accomplish great things. Be empowered to live life unlimited!

TABLE OF CONTENTS

BE ACTIVE

"A year from now, you may wish you had started today."
~Karen Lamb, Author

Allison was very talented at baking and had inherited her grandmother's secret recipes. While she worked as an office assistant, her dream was to open her own bakery in the downtown district where she lived. There had not been a local bakery in the area for years and Allison believed it was a perfect spot. Allison often baked pies and cakes for office parties and holiday events. During a holiday party, a co-worker introduced her to an investment banker who was incredibly impressed with Allison's desserts. When Allison told the banker about her dream of owning a bakery, he encouraged her to fill out an application for a small business loan. He gave Allison his card and told her to schedule a meeting with him the following week. Allison met with the banker, who ultimately decided to invest in her business and helped her get her bakery up and running. Today, Allison owns a successful bakery in the downtown district of her hometown.

In the hypothetical above, Allison did several things right. First, she was willing to start small by baking for office parties and holiday events. Second, she was not afraid to share her dream of owning a bakery. Because she shared her dream, her co-worker was able to connect Allison with someone who could assist her. Finally, when Allison had an opportunity to move forward, she followed through with it. She met with the banker the next week, which led to Allison opening her bakery.

No one ever achieved her dream by standing still in one place. One of the main reasons people do not

1

fulfill their dreams is because they are not willing to do what it takes to make the dream a reality. Dreams are simply goals you have yet to put into action. In order to make the dream a reality, you have to actually do something.

Have you ever heard someone talk about wanting to change a job? Have you ever been around someone who wished they had a bigger home or better car? Have you ever listened to someone complain about his life with the dream of living a better one? I have been around all of these people and unfortunately, for many of them, a year will pass by and they will still be talking about the job, house, car, and life they want to have without having taken any steps toward making it happen.

While pregnant with my son, Tristan, I gained fifty pounds. If you have never been pregnant before, let me just tell you, fifty pounds is a lot of weight. In general, I have a small frame and have always been a fairly small size. Throughout my life, I have consistently engaged in some form of exercise, whether it was walking, running, or going to the gym. I even worked out five days a week up until the week before I had Tristan. Naturally, I wanted to return to my regular size shortly after giving birth. Although much of the weight was water weight, which I lost pretty quickly, for over a year, I was still ten pounds over my pre-pregnancy weight. What did I do?

I jumped into action. I committed to being more consistent with my workout, including using videos and my in-home elliptical machine. I became more conscious of what I was eating and the time of day I was eating it. For example, I needed carbs because I was doing a lot of cardio and strength training. However, I made sure to have most of my carbs earlier in the day rather than for dinner. I was used to eating a salad (It's my favorite snack☺) each day after work. Due to my busy schedule, I was often eating a high calorie meal late at night, after I put Tristan down. Instead, I began eating my dinner during the same time I fed Tristan. When I felt hungry later, I had my favorite snack – a salad. Miraculously, the weight began to disappear and I was finally able to fit back into my skinny jeans!

Of course, what I did was no miracle. It really wasn't anything abnormal or extraordinary. I had a goal which was not going to accomplish itself. When I decided to get active, I began to see a change. Too often, people want something to happen, but they do not realize they have to make it happen. It is good to set goals. In fact, I would argue setting goals is essential to living your life unlimited. However, setting a goal is only the first step to seeing it become a reality. You cannot simply set the goal and wish it into existence. Once you set the goal, you have to develop a plan for how you will accomplish it. Then, you must get to work.

Although setting high goals is important, it is equally important to write your goals down where you can see them. I knew the title of my first book long before I finished writing the book. As a form of inspiration, I wrote the title on a piece of paper, along with my weekly writing goals for completing the book. I placed the paper on my refrigerator so each time I opened the door, I would see my goals and be reminded of what I needed to accomplish.

Writing the goals down and placing the paper on my refrigerator was only the first step. I actually had to sit down and write on a consistent basis in order to finish the book. Several times a year, I am approached by aspiring writers. They share their goals and I offer whatever advice I can to motivate them. However, more times than not, when I see them again, they are still aspiring writers. I have often heard the difference between winners and losers is winners are willing to do things losers will not do. If you are not willing to get moving, you will not see your dreams come to fruition.

When I am writing a book, it can take months or even years to complete. The writing process is long and arduous. The revision process can be tedious. When I am writing, there are many days I want to come home from work and take a nap or zone out watching a good movie. However, I cannot expect to do what I feel like doing each day and still accomplish my goal. Some days I need to pull away from my writing to reboot my creativity. When I need to be refreshed and re-energized, I go to the beach or spend time with my family. Once I feel revived and recharged, I am back to writing on schedule because the book is not going to write itself. We all know Dr. Martin Luther King Jr. had a dream. However, Dr. King also had to march, give speeches, participate in protests, and inspire others in order to make the dream a reality. What makes you any different?

You will always have distractions which have the potential to pull you away from finishing the task you are trying to complete. Some of your challenges may include household duties, money woes, family responsibilities, time management, friends who want to hangout, health concerns, personal issues, work-related stress, sleep deprivation, or a lack of motivation. Any one of the challenges listed can derail your plan to get moving and stay active. Just know there will be sacrifices you must make in order to reach your end result. Some days your house may not be spotless. Other days, you may be running on a few hours of sleep. Sometimes your family may have to eat leftovers. The key is to balance the sacrifices across the board so no single area is completely ignored. When you finally achieve what you aimed to do, it will be well worth it.

It also helps to share your goals with people who want to see you succeed. Their encouragement can help keep you focused on your goal. When I tell my husband about a new project I want to start, he will often make suggestions about it or help me brainstorm while I am planning. As the project progresses, he will undoubtedly ask questions or provide feedback. His support is beneficial because it helps keep me motivated. It is also useful to surround yourself with other people who are actively pursuing their goals. I call them "accountability partners." When you align yourself with people who understand the time commitment and necessary discipline involved, it is an added layer of support to help ensure your success. My cousin, Neca, has been my accountability partner for years. Although we do not have a set schedule to meet and discuss our endeavors, we regularly check in with one another about our goals and the progress we are making. Because I know she is going to ask about what I am doing or upcoming activities in which I may be involved, it helps keep me focused. No one likes to be the weakest link, and I am no exception. When she asks, I want to be able to say I'm working toward accomplishing a goal I have set.

There will always be great temptation to wait and get started tomorrow. When I was younger, my great-grandmother would tell me not to put off until tomorrow what I could do today. I encourage you to avoid procrastination at all costs. In my experience, every dream requires action to become a reality. You will never get from here to there by simply talking about it. You have to actually do something. Don't wait another minute. Stop talking about it and be about it. Take the first step you need toward making your dream a reality and keep moving!

BE ACTIVE REFLECTION

❖ Identify one short term goal and one long term goal you want to achieve. Why are the goals important to you? What resources (time, money, materials, or people) will you need to accomplish the goals?

❖ Consider an important goal you achieved in the past. How were you able to accomplish the goal? What steps can you take now to ensure you are able to accomplish the goals you have today?

❖ Think about the obstacles which potentially stand in the way of you achieving your goals. What can you do to be proactive and prevent the obstacles from becoming a hindrance?

BE BALANCED

*"Balance is not something you find. It's
something you create."*
~Jana Kingsford, Australian Blogger

  *The cruise ship was Carnival Valor. It was a week-
long trip to Honduras, Belize, Grand Cayman, and
Mexico. As soon as I stepped aboard the ship, I felt as if
two tons of bricks had been lifted off my shoulders. I was
free! There were no emails to check. All voicemails
would have to wait. My biggest priority in the moment
was getting my sail away drink and sailing away.*
  *For seven days, my husband and I laughed way
too much and ate even more. We stayed up late and
slept in whenever we wanted. We filled our days by
touring other countries and participating in different
excursions. However, at the end of our amazing trip,
instead of feeling refreshed and ready to take on the next
few months, a deep feeling of dread set in. For one week,
we had been drifting on a virtual utopian paradise, for
which we had no frame of reference in our actual daily
lives. We knew once we departed the ship, it would not
take long for us to settle back into the hectic hustle and
bustle of every day. The first time I spent seven days on
a cruise ship, I realized taking time to unplug and unwind
is as essential to my life as air. Since taking a cruise
every other month was not an option, I had to learn to
incorporate the principles of cruising into my lifestyle.*
  I have often heard people refer to happiness as
being more of a journey than a final destination. For me,
achieving balance is very similar. Finding a happy
median between all of the priorities in life is a challenge
for most people. If you work hard at your job or career,

8

you will likely be praised for your efforts. However, your relationships with family and friends may suffer because of the long hours you put in at the office. If you choose investing time in your relationships over taking on a special project or extra hours at work, you may not advance as quickly or may feel unsatisfied professionally.

Women, especially, seem to struggle with work life balance because of societal expectations and standards. Women are often made to feel as if they must choose between their aspirations. Love or career? Career or family? Status or happiness? In reality, it is possible to do it all, just not at the same time. If you have balance, you can find satisfaction in all facets of life. The challenge is learning how to live in balance.

Setting and respecting boundaries is key to maintaining balance in your life. In Ecclesiastes 3:1, the scripture says, "There is a time for everything, and a season for every activity under the heavens." If there is a time to work, there must be a time to rest. Unfortunately, many people spend too much time at one end of the spectrum, leaving their lives in disarray.

If you work, there is generally a start time and a stop time. How you honor those boundaries is a conscious decision with real consequences. For example, if your work hours are generally from 8:00 a.m. to 5:00 p.m., you may still have unfinished work at 5:00 p.m. Depending on your job, you will have to decide if the unfinished work can wait until the next day or if it must be finished immediately. If it must be finished immediately, can it be done at the office or should you take it home? Likewise, if you sit around and watch unlimited amounts of television, you will not likely accomplish your goals. You cannot spend all your time leisurely and expect important tasks to get done on their own. There has to be some balance between work and play.

For many people, much time is spent on social media and electronic devices. If you do not consciously monitor the time you spend on electronic devices and online, it could have a negative effect on your personal interaction with others. It is not uncommon to go to dinner and observe a couple rarely interact with one another. Although they may be sitting across from each other, their eyes are often glued to their phones. While the advantages of technology make life easier in many ways, it can also complicate how you balance your life.

Years ago, if someone tried to reach you and you did not answer the phone, they had to leave a message and wait for you to return the call. Now, people have an all access pass to your life through social media. Because you own a mobile phone, people have a greater expectation for you to answer their call, despite your schedule.   Setting boundaries for when you will check your email or post information on social media may help you achieve greater balance. For example, my husband and I do not access our phones for the internet or social media when we are out with each other. The point of spending time together is to enjoy one another's company. If we spend it checking social media posts, we have wasted time.

Likewise, there should be a cutoff time when you disconnect from all electronic devices to give yourself a break. I do not usually take my phone with me to the gym because I want to get an uninterrupted workout. Additionally, I rarely know where my phone is during the weekend because I am generally with my family doing family activities. While your job may require you to be more accessible, you can certainly set limitations.

I do not know a working individual who has not had to stay late or work after hours at some point. However, if staying late is your norm rather than the exception, you may be out of balance. Admittedly, I was guilty of spending too much time working. As a high school teacher, I usually stayed late to grade papers, create assignments, or get organized for the next day. Unfortunately, instead of feeling accomplished, I often left feeling cranky and annoyed because leaving work late shifted the rest of my schedule. Even though I had other responsibilities, I was making work the main priority. After leaving work late, I was rushing to stop by the grocery store or picking up my child later than I expected. I was not making it to the gym or meeting my writing goals as often as I had planned. I rarely ever had the chance to just go home and rest after work, and it did not leave me feeling very happy.

Eventually, I realized there will always be work to do. Instead of trying to get it all done at once, I began to prioritize. If it could wait until the next day, it had to wait. I started setting time limits for myself and forcing myself out of the building. Realistically, I knew there would be days I needed to stay late for meetings or other duties. However, I tried to plan ahead for those days and stick to my boundaries. Overall, I felt much happier and more productive.

We each get twenty-four hours in a day. You control how you utilize the hours of your day. Even if you were given more hours, it would not help you if you are not using the time you already have wisely. There is a difference between being busy and being productive. You can be involved in activities, spend long hours at the office, and still not be productive. You can do volunteer work, spend time helping others in need, and still be out of balance. Sometimes what you are doing may be good, but not necessarily good for you. If it is not what you are designed to be doing in the given season of your life, it may not produce any fruit and leave you feeling unproductive and unfulfilled.

My family is my priority, and the time I invest in my personal relationships matters. Therefore, I have to be intentional about how I divide my time working on my personal goals and the amount of time I spend nurturing the relationships in my life. During an interview, television producer, Shonda Rhimes, shared a best practice for living in balance. As the creator of several award-winning television shows, such as *Grey's Anatomy* and *How to Get Away With Murder*, she undoubtedly has a busy schedule. Yet, anytime her kids ask her to play with them, she takes a moment to do it. After hearing her share this best practice, I began to incorporate it into my routine. No matter how busy I am, if my child asks me to play with him, I find time to do it, if only for a moment. It reminds me to stop and appreciate the small blessings in life, like laughing with my son. It also helps me to remember all work and no play leads to an imbalanced lifestyle.

You are not a one dimensional creature, but rather complex and compound. Therefore, it is important to nurture all aspects of your well-being. Do the important people in your life complain about the lack of time you have for them? Are you frustrated because you miss important events involving family or friends? If your answer is yes, take time to re-evaluate how you distribute your time and energy. Five years from now, will you be happy with how you spent your time or will you wish you had it back?

Greek author, Laertius Diogenes, said "Time is the most valuable thing a man can spend." No one ever makes a dying declaration to have one more day of work or more time to post on social media. Make sure you take time for the people who are important to you and the activities which make you happy. Each day, you should do something you enjoy, whether it's exercising, having breakfast with your spouse, practicing a new hobby, meeting a friend for lunch, heading to the spa, or soaking in a nice, hot bubble bath. You only get one life to live. Make sure you are living it to its fullest!

BE BALANCED REFLECTION

❖ Think about your work-life balance. In what area(s) of your life do you need to work on maintaining more balance? What are the challenges you face when trying to maintain balance in your life?

❖ Consider how you spend each day. What effect would a more balanced lifestyle have on you and your relationships? Identify two changes you can make to ensure you have a more balanced life.

❖ For the next two weeks, make a commitment to incorporate the changes into your daily routine. Keep a journal about your experience. At the end of the two weeks, evaluate whether the changes made a difference.

BE COMMITTED

"Once you have commitment, you need the discipline
and hard work to get you there."
~Haile Gebrselassie, Olympic Athlete and Medalist

"Do you run?" I asked.

I had not been running in months, but I still really enjoyed it. For me, running had become a great workout and a good stress reliever.

"Yes, do you?" Melissa asked.

We were having lunch and getting to know one another while working on a project for our school district.

"I do, but it's been a while," I told her.

"You should run this 5K with me. It's in February, so you have plenty of time to train. And, it's for a good cause – homelessness!" Melissa said excitedly.

"Okay! I'm in!" I said without any hesitation. It was a great way for me to start running again and for a cause near and dear to my heart.

Over the next several months, Melissa and I exchanged text messages, emails, and phone calls. We updated one another on our conditioning progress. There were times when I ran three to four times per week. However, there were some weeks when I could only run once or twice.

A few days before the race, I could feel my sinuses acting up. Since it happens several times a year, I knew I was getting a sinus infection. Sure enough, the night before the race, I was at the local drugstore clinic trying to get a prescription for a post nasal drip that was making me miserable. By the time I went to bed, there were only about five hours before I needed to be up again. Unfortunately, the medicine I took made me sleepy, and

I overslept. Then, the meteorologist reported it was in the low 40s. I was feeling horrible, and I really didn't want to have my two-year-old out in the cold weather. Needless to say, I had plenty of excuses not to go to the race. But, I had made a commitment, and I intended to keep it.

Determined not to be defeated before I even began, I pulled myself together and made it to the race. I completed my first 5K feeling sleep deprived, with a sinus infection, in cold weather, and on prescription medication. Now, that's commitment!

When you first set a goal, you likely have the intention of accomplishing it. What you do in the days, weeks, and months in between will determine whether it happens. There were plenty of reasons for me not to run the morning of the 5K. They were not irrational excuses, but rather viable reasons to stay home. However, it was more important for me to honor my commitment and accomplish the goal. During the race, I barely thought about my sinus infection. I was so energized by the commitment of those around me; I paid little attention to how I was feeling or the cold weather. My son was wrapped up in layers and made it through without a sniffle. When I crossed the finish line, I was proud I had stayed the course and finished the race.

When people give up, it is often the result of fear or unrealistic estimations of time, energy, and sacrifice. Sometimes, people are afraid of failure and success. If they fail, they might be embarrassed or have to explain their mistakes. If they succeed, people might expect more of them. If you engage in enough negative self-talk, you can talk yourself out of just about anything.

I could never start my own business. I don't have the money. I can't go back to school. It's been too long. I'll never lose weight. I don't have time to exercise. These statements are common excuses people make when they are afraid to commit. You may fear failure if you have a hard time visualizing yourself succeeding. If you set the goal, but cannot imagine yourself crossing the finish line, you probably will not get in the race. Additionally, if the negative self-talk is more dominant than the positive self-talk, you are unlikely to remain committed. You have to silence negativity and eradicate excuses if you want to remain committed to your goals.

It is important to commit yourself to things for which you have connection, passion, or enthusiasm. If you are committed through connection, you may be doing something because someone close to you asked a favor. It may be a part of your job duty to complete the task. Or, you may be helping someone in need. You do not have to necessarily enjoy what you do in order to be dedicated to the task. When you decide not to allow your feelings to control your decisions, it is possible to be committed, even when you feel like being uncommitted. If you volunteer to give a co-worker a ride to and from work while his car is being fixed, honor your word. If you wake up late one morning or would rather leave early, you should first consider the commitment. After a few days, you may grow tired of going out of your way to pick him up and take him home. However, when you commit yourself to something, you are saying, "You can depend on me!"

Years ago, I wanted to be a criminal profiler and applied to the FBI. As a part of the application process, I was required to pass a physical fitness test. Two of the requirements were a 300 meter sprint and a one and a half mile run. When I first began running, I had no interest in it other than meeting the requirement. I could barely run a lap without being out of breath. I was a cheerleader in high school and was active throughout college. I often went walking with my girlfriends and sometimes worked out at the gym. However, running was different. I did not understand how to control my breathing. I had no idea how to step heel to toe. You could hear me stomping a mile away. I was literally, all over the place. After weeks of training with a more experienced athlete, I began to see progress. After a few months of running five to six days a week, I was running four miles with ease. I ran whether it was hot, cold, or raining. I ran whether I felt like it or not. I even ran on Christmas morning when everyone else was opening gifts. I was deeply committed to accomplishing my goal. For several weeks, I actually ran at 4:00 a.m. prior to going to work, which really took commitment because I was not a morning person.

At the time, I did not particularly enjoy running, especially early in the morning. However, my feelings had nothing to do with my level of commitment to passing the physical fitness test. I understood it to be a necessary sacrifice for the goal I was seeking to accomplish. While I passed the physical fitness test and entered the FBI Academy, I ultimately decided I did not want to be an FBI Agent. However, going through the process of training for the Academy was a game-changer for me.

Many people fail to make it to the finish line because they are unwilling to make the necessary sacrifices. No matter what your dream may be, it is going to cost you something. The most common sacrifices you will have to make are time and money. When I wrote my first book, *Unlimit Yourself*, I was newly married and working a full-time job. At the time, it was just me and my husband – no kids or dog. Three to four times a week, I left work and went directly to the public library. I setup my laptop in one of the quiet study rooms and wrote for hours until the library closed. On weekends, I spent hours at the library or local coffee shops writing, proofreading, and revising. I followed the routine for months until my book was finished. There were days when my husband had to pull me away from the computer. Surely, I did not always feel like writing. Some days, the words which made it on the page were not so impressive. However, I was committed to the process. While it meant having to temporarily sacrifice sleep and personal time, it was necessary to finish the book.

What if I told you it would take twenty years before you would see your dream become a reality? Would you still pursue it? Would you give up after a couple of years? We definitely live in a microwave society. People want what they want and they want it now. Though some dreams may not take twenty years to fulfill, they still may not happen quite as fast as you would hope. I felt an enthusiasm and love for writing at an early age. I first attempted to write a book when I was in the fourth grade, but did not publish my first book until twenty years later. While I pursued other endeavors, I never gave up on my dream of writing a book. I was committed to seeing it through.

I wear a necklace with a turtle pendant because it reminds me about the story of the tortoise and the hare. The tortoise and the hare were involved in a race. Although the tortoise was much slower than the hare, the hare wanted to take shortcuts and even slept, while the tortoise consistently plodded along. While the hare was sleeping, the tortoise crossed the finish line and beat his opponent, who was much faster. Whenever I am tempted to rush through the process, I remember the lesson – *Slow and steady wins the race.*

When it comes to realizing your dreams, you should be like a pit bull in a fight. Go in knowing it will take more time and energy than you imagined. The most successful people in life are those who understand the price of success. Will it take longer than you expected? Possibly. However, the time is going to pass anyway. You might as well come out of it having achieved your aspirations. Will it cost you something financially? More than likely. It is called investing in yourself.

You cannot move to the next level without the help of others. You may need to attend classes, workshops, seminars, and conferences to achieve your dream. You might have to buy books and other materials to assist you. If it will help you get to the finish line, it is worth it. Remain committed to the process and refuse to give up. As Forest Whitaker stated in the movie, *The Great Debaters*, "We do what we have to do in order to do what we want to do!"

BE COMMITTED REFLECTION

❖ Think of a time when you made a commitment and saw it through to the end. What was the outcome? How did it make you feel?

❖ What is one area in your life where you need to be more committed? Explain why you feel a deeper level of commitment is needed in this area of your life.

❖ What are some obstacles which prevent you from being as committed as you need to be? Explain what you can do to overcome these obstacles.

BE DILIGENT

"Hard work beats talent when talent doesn't work hard."
~Tim Notke, High School Basketball Coach

When I graduated from law school, I had to take the Florida Bar Exam to become a licensed attorney. We had a common saying among the law students in my class –Respect the bar! We all understood our intellect alone would not be enough to pass the bar exam. There was too much information to learn and little time to learn it. There was no way to get around putting in the time and effort it took to study for the two day test.

For almost three months, I studied ten to twelve hours per day. On any given night, my living room floor was littered with sixteen books on various types of law. Torts. Contracts. Civil Procedure. Criminal Law. Each day, I followed the same routine. Eat. Study. Study. Study. Sleep. Repeat. During those months, my priority was to pass the test. I became an expert at multi-tasking and after six years of college, finally mastered the art of studying. Fortunately, the effort paid off and I passed the bar exam on my first attempt.

It is difficult to discuss diligence without mentioning commitment and discipline because most people who work hard are usually committed and practice self-control. You may not always feel like your efforts are appreciated or like your hard work is paying off. Remember, however, those who finish first do not necessarily finish best. It is important to appreciate the process because there is much to be learned from it.

Two years after I began teaching in South Florida, I was voted as Teacher of the Year for the high school at which I was teaching. It was an honor because it said my colleagues thought I was doing a great job and recognized my hard work and dedication. One day after the vote, my assistant principal informed me I could not be Teacher of the Year because I had not been in the school district for more than three years. However, he offered to award me with Rookie Teacher of the Year, which was for teachers with less than three years teaching experience. Since I had taught for two years in a different school district, I did not feel it was fair for me to assume the Rookie Teacher of the Year title. Therefore, I declined his offer. I continued to work hard, staying late after school, working on weekends, and going the extra mile. No one was really asking me to do any of those things. However, I had a certain standard and expectation, not only for my students, but for myself, as well. There was no way to get the job done without going beyond what was required.

Nine years after my first nomination, I was voted Teacher of the Year again, but at a different school. Wouldn't you know it was two years after I began? I did not stop working as hard or put in less effort when the first award was rescinded because the award was not my motivation for working hard. Having a strong work ethic is a state of mind and must become a part of your fabric. It has to be a non-negotiable if you want to live your dream. If the amount of effort you are willing to give is based only on the immediate payoff, prepare to live life frustrated and disappointed.

There is motivation for everything you do. If you exercise, the motivation may be to lose weight and feel better about yourself. If you eat healthy, the motivation might be to improve your overall health and live longer. If you budget, the motivation may be to live a comfortable lifestyle and take annual vacations. If you are currently in school, the motivation may be to earn a degree and get a better paying job. Regardless of your motivation, you will not get from the starting point to the finish line without putting forth maximum effort and staying focused on your goal.

It may seem like those who put forth little effort are the ones who get promoted or receive all the breaks. However, as Polonius said in Shakespeare's *Hamlet*, "To thine own self be true." Even if the people around you are slacking off, you should still work hard and give your best effort. Their assignment in life might be different than yours. They may not have the same dreams and goals as you. They might not need to learn the same lessons because they are not headed to the same place. If you are watching someone else, make sure you are following a good example. Do not allow someone who is taking shortcuts and looking for an easy way out to be your role model. If you need inspiration or an example to follow, make sure it is someone who always gives her best and never settles for doing just the bare minimum.

Years ago, I ran into a co-worker at the start of the day. Walking from the parking lot, we greeted each other and made small talk about our weekend. As we begin to wrap up our conversation, I smiled and said, "Well, you have a good day."

My co-worker replied, "Oh, you know me. I'm not working too hard. All I do is chill. So, every day is a good day."

Immediately, I cringed. All day, my co-worker's words haunted me. I could not understand why I was so bothered, but I had definitely been affected by our exchange. Initially, I thought it was because I knew I would not be chilling, as there was too much work to be done. I thought to myself, *Am I jealous? Is it because I wish I could say the same?*

A few weeks later, I realized I was so upset by my co-worker's words because I understand the importance of hard work. To me, it appeared my co-worker was not being diligent or giving his best. Even if I wanted to have a lackadaisical attitude, I never could because it is not who I am. I am not made from lackadaisical fabric. I know my purpose, and the dreams I have require me to work hard and give my best effort each day. My dreams certainly are not going to come true without me being diligent.

You will always find people who are looking to do less than everyone else. There is no shortage of people who have a dream but are unwilling to do what it takes to make the dream a reality. In most cases, success rarely happens according to your timeline. When you see successful people, you are often viewing the finished product. It is rare to see the process from start to finish. As a result, it can be easy to think success just fell from the sky. More than likely, the successful person you are watching worked hard for the success he achieved.

Rapper and entrepreneur, Jay–Z, a.k.a. Shawn Carter, was in the music industry for almost twenty years before he became a breakout star and experienced musical success. I remember because I actually liked his verse as a guest rapper on the song, "Hawaiian Sophie." There are not many people who would wait twenty years to see a dream come true or work for twenty years to perfect a craft. Most people would have given up or certainly would have become discouraged. His story is a great example of how working hard and putting forth the effort brings reward.

Prolific author, Stephen King, received so many rejection letters from publishers he reportedly threw his manuscript for the book, *Carrie,* in the trash. However, his diligence and unwillingness to give up made him one of the more successful and memorable authors in the entertainment industry. Many of his books, including *Carrie*, have been made into successful and critically acclaimed motion pictures. Like Stephen King, your success may not come the first time or second time you try. You may have to work harder, stay longer, and practice more than those around you. It may take longer than you expected. However, remain diligent. Those who experience lasting success are usually those who put in the work ahead of time.

I love an underdog story, possibly because I consider myself to be an underdog. According to statistics, I should not be college educated, married, or in the position to accomplish the things I have in life. I was born to a teenage mother, who battled drug addiction for years. I was raised by my great-grandparents and grew up without knowing my biological father. Because of my family history, I learned the importance of being diligent and faithful in small things.

When you work for what you have, you appreciate it more. While many of my friends were fortunate to have their parents buy them cars, I was not. I did not purchase my first car until I was about to graduate from college. I worked at the Florida State University Credit Union and saved my money to make the down payment. After purchasing the car, there were times I worked two jobs to make my car payment. Long after I paid the car off and could have purchased a newer model, I kept it because it held sentimental value. I kept the car in good condition by washing it and making sure the oil was changed regularly. Sixteen years and almost 300,000 miles later, I sold it to a family in need of a second vehicle. While it would have been nice to receive a car on my sixteenth birthday, I know my first car meant more to me because I worked hard for it.

You can be smart, but intellect will only take you so far. You can network with others, but those connections will only get you into the door. At some point, you must be willing to put in the work. I will take someone with a strong work ethic over raw talent any day because raw talent needs to be developed to move to the next level. Without a strong work ethic, talent will remain at surface level and never reach its full potential.

BE DILIGENT REFLECTION

❖ What are the characteristics of a hard worker? On a scale of 1 to 10, with 1 being the lowest and 10 being the highest, rate yourself based on the characteristics you listed.

❖ Think of a time when you reaped the rewards of hard work. What was the situation and how did you feel about the outcome?

❖ What is one area in your life where you need to be more diligent? Explain how you can improve in this area of your life.

BE EXPECTANT

"Whether you think you can or you think you can't,
you're right."
~Henry Ford, American Inventor

When I was in high school, the Silver Garland Award was the most prestigious award given to high school seniors in our county. There were ten categories, including math, music, art, and citizenship, in which students completed special projects and activities in an effort to improve their community. Each year, one senior could be nominated in each category per school. The nominees competed against one another and participated in a panel interview with business leaders from the community. As a senior, I was nominated for citizenship.

To date, my Silver Garland interview is probably one of the worst interviews I have ever had. I can remember stumbling over words and having a difficult time expressing my ideas. I walked out of the interview feeling as if I had lost any chance of winning the award. Growing up, my great-grandmother attended every award ceremony for which I was a nominee. However, I told her she did not need to attend the Silver Garland Award Ceremony because I was certain I would not win. She decided to attend anyway.

On the day of the ceremony, I rode with my friend, who was nominated in the art category. We were in no rush to arrive early because we were sure neither of us had won. In fact, we took our time and stopped by a fast food restaurant on the way to the ceremony. Since Silver Garland was such a prestigious honor, it was a highly publicized, formal event. We arrived just before the ceremony was starting and had to be rushed onstage by one of the organizers. The mistress of ceremonies went through each category by giving a highlight of the projects the nominees had completed. Then, she read a detailed description of the winner's accolades and accomplishments before announcing the winner's name.

In my category, there were students who had traveled to other countries to assist in missions trips. My activities included working with my church and community center to provide an afterschool tutoring program for younger students and helping organize a community breakfast. When the mistress of ceremonies began to list the attributes of the winner in my category, I thought it sounded a lot like me. The winner was a varsity cheerleader, as was I. The winner had also been voted "Most Likely to Succeed," similar to me. It was not until I heard the winner had won "The Woodsman of the World History Award" that I realized it was me. I had won the Silver Garland Award! Of all the awards I have received, an award I received in high school is the one for which I am most proud because I did not expect to receive it.

Winning Silver Garland taught me an important life lesson. If I had not attended the ceremony, the award would have been given to the runner-up. I almost missed out on receiving a prestigious award and scholarship just because I did not expect to win. No matter what the situation appears to be, you should always expect the best outcome. Even if the worst happens, you will not be worse off for having expected the best.

In life, you have the opportunity to expect good things to happen in your life as much as you have the opportunity to expect bad things to happen. It is all dependent upon your personal outlook. There are some people who expect heartache, calamity, and trouble to occur in their lives. While we all face challenges, some people seem to always have one bad break after another. If you are one of those people, I would challenge you to examine what you are expecting to happen in your life. How would you evaluate your thought life? Are you expecting bad breaks? Do you believe your current situation is an accurate depiction of your future? Or, are you expecting negative situations to turn around in your favor?

Some people prefer not to set high expectations because they fear being disappointed. They make a decision not to get their hopes up or feel too passionate about anything in an effort to avoid getting their feelings hurt or being let down. While no one enjoys be disappointed, you cannot go through life without facing disappointments, setbacks, or failure. Even if there is a chance the situation may not go your way, it is better to expect the best than to give in and accept defeat before you know the outcome. Hope does not cost you anything, but it does involve effort because faith requires you to believe and walk in your belief.

In the Bible, Mark 5: 25-34, there is a story about a woman who suffered from a blood disease for twelve years. She had spent all her money going to doctors, but none were able to cure her of the disease. As a result of her disease, the people considered her to be unclean and unfit to be among a crowd. However, when she heard Jesus was passing through her town, she risked everything to get close to Him. She was expecting a miracle! She believed if she could just touch a part of the clothing Jesus was wearing, she would be healed. Courageously, she made her way through the large crowd and got close enough to touch the hem of His robe.

According to the scripture, Jesus felt her touch him, even in the vast crowd. Jesus not only healed the woman, but He acknowledged it was her faith which made her well. She received the healing because she expected to receive it and was willing to act with expectancy.

The man who lives his life expecting to face challenges, will consistently face challenges. The man who does not expect to be successful in life, will not be successful. What are you expecting to happen in your life? Are you expecting healing? Do you anticipate promotion? Do you envision doors of opportunity opening up in your life? I recently had a conversation with a high school student regarding his future. As a ninth grade gifted and honors student, he was already visualizing his failure. When I asked him about college, he told me he wanted to go to a major university, but he knew he would never get in. No matter how much I tried to encourage him and convince him it was possible, he was certain it would not happen. As we discussed financial aid, he informed me he would never get any scholarships. Despite my efforts, he had decided he was not going to expect much so he would not be let down. If there was a battle going on in his mind, he was losing the battle by accepting defeat before really even getting started.

If you live in South Florida for more than a year, you will become an expert on hurricane preparedness. If the meteorologist announces there is a hurricane approaching the South Florida area, people flock to the nearest station to fill up their tanks. You may see a line of cars for several miles waiting to get gas. It is not uncommon for stations to run out of gasoline. Residents stock up on water, non-perishable foods, flashlights, and other necessities. People put up hurricane shutters to protect their homes from damage and bring in items which could be tossed around in the wind. Once the necessary precautions have been taken, many people make a decision to wait out the storm. In other words, they wait in expectancy for it to arrive. There are some people, however, who take steps to prepare for the storm, but continue their daily routine, expecting the storm to bypass them. To which category would you belong?

As adults, we allow past disappointments to impact how we view the future. Instead of always expecting the best or remembering when things worked out in our favor, we recall all the times we felt let down. Children are different. They naturally expect good things to happen to them. They believe Santa, The Easter Bunny, mommy, daddy, and grandma want to give them toys and treats. Last Christmas, my son, Tristan, went through the toy store advertisement and confidently pointed out each toy he wanted. He was bold in asking and fully expected to receive what he wanted. Although he did not receive anywhere near the number of toys he pointed out, it will hardly discourage him from asking for what he wants in the future.

Not long ago, Tristan told me he wanted a baby brother or baby sister. Although my husband and I would love to expand our family, it is not something either of us had discussed with him.

One day, as Tristan and I were walking to the car, he asked, "Mommy, did God bring us a baby yet?"

I was quite surprised, and responded, "Not, yet."

A few minutes later, I asked, "Tristan, do you want God to bring us a baby?"

He smiled and said excitedly, "Yes, mommy! You must never give up!"

I was astounded by the boldness of his declaration.

33

"Tristan, who told you to never give up?" I asked curiously.

"Jesus!" he responded.

Later that night, Tristan and I prayed for God to send us a baby. Even though it has not happened yet, I choose to have bold faith like that of my four-year-old son. I am expecting only the best!

BE EXPECTANT REFLECTION

❖ Identify something for which you are waiting for with great expectancy.

❖ How can you maintain hope when nothing is happening? What can you do to demonstrate an attitude of expectancy?

❖ How do you handle disappointment? What steps can you take to ensure your disappointments do not hinder you in the future?

BE FIREPROOF

"If you are going through hell, keep going."
~Winston Churchill, Former British Prime Minister

Karen was a single mother, raising two kids, and working two jobs just to make ends meet. When her apartment manager told her he would be increasing the rent on her small apartment, it could not have been worse timing. Earlier in the week, she had learned one of her jobs would be laying off more than a third of the employees. Unfortunately, Karen was among those who would be let go. Rather than panic, Karen began to pray and decided to inform her apartment manager of the possible layoff. To her surprise, the manager asked if she would be interested in applying for an assistant office manager position with the company. Within two weeks, Karen was offered the job, which paid substantially more than the job she had before. As an employee with the company, she received a discount on her rent. After a year, Karen received a promotion and was able to quit her second job.

In the scenario, Karen could have become negative about her situation. She could have complained to the apartment manager it wasn't fair for her to have to pay more for her rent. Karen could have felt sorry for herself and expected others to do the same. She could have easily given up and said, *Nothing good ever happens to me. It's just my luck.*

Instead, Karen chose to move forward with a positive attitude expecting everything to work in her favor. When you decide to be fireproof, you decide not to allow the fires in life to destroy you. Yes, it is a choice!

One of the more popular lines from the movie, *Forrest Gump,* is "Life is like a box of chocolates. You never know what you're going to get." You cannot predict or prevent all the challenges you will face in life. When you face your most difficult circumstances, your true character is revealed. When diamonds are formed, they must undergo high levels of pressure and endure high temperatures. The end result of withstanding the extremely high temperatures is a precious gem admired by most. The term, "diamond in the rough" is often used to describe someone or something having the potential to be excellent and showing promise for greatness. The rough part is a reference to the need for more development or growth in a particular area.

Diamond people are those who do not crack under the pressures of life, but rather come through the fire shining brighter than ever. My great-grandmother, Thelma Battle (Mama), is what I consider a diamond person. As a child, she lost a younger sibling when he was accidentally run over by a car. When Mama was only twelve years old, her mother died while giving birth. Consequently, she and her siblings were raised by their maternal grandmother. Not wanting to live under the strict rules of her grandmother, Mama married soon after her high school graduation. Unfortunately, it was a physically abusive relationship and Mama chose to leave her husband while she was pregnant with her second child. She eventually remarried and had a third child.

Mama's second husband (Daddy), my great-grandfather and the only real father in my life, was a great provider. Daddy was kind, generous, and raised Mama's children, grandchildren, and great grandchildren as his own. However, he was not always faithful in marriage. Unfortunately, Daddy's extramarital affairs were a source of great sadness and heartache for Mama. Yet, she remained in the marriage and was a dutiful wife, lovingly caring for him up until his death due to cancer. Perhaps, however, the greatest heartache Mama suffered was when her only son was shot and killed by police during a robbery. After having experienced tremendous loss in her life, Mama faced another personal battle when she was diagnosed with colon cancer in 2006. Ever the resilient gem, she had surgery and has been cancer-free for over ten years.

At ninety-five, she still lives an active and vibrant life. While she has been through unimaginable challenges, her experiences did not make her bitter. She does not complain about how hard her life has been or the difficulties she faced. She is not angry for the hurts and disappointments she experienced. Instead, she celebrates having come through the fire stronger and more brilliant than ever. She exemplifies what it means to live a diamond life.

Do not allow your circumstances to get the best of you. Maybe you lost a job or were passed over for a promotion. Perhaps you were betrayed by a friend or someone you loved. It is hurtful when your plans do not work out the way you hoped. It can be especially painful when those close to you mistreat or disappoint you. However, you only hurt yourself by allowing a negative situation to turn you into a negative person. It is easy to look at people who are seemingly happy and assume their lives have been easy. Much like you, even celebrities, who appear to be living fabulous lives, have to go through the fire.

Jennifer Hudson won *American Idol*, became a successful singer, and received an Oscar for her performance in the movie, *Dreamgirls*. During what was likely one of the most exciting times in her life, her world was rocked to the core. Her sister's ex-husband shot and killed her mother and nephew. Kanye West, a talented lyricist and multimillionaire, lost his mother when she died unexpectedly from complications following plastic surgery. Rihanna is arguably one of the most influential pop culture icons of the 2010s. However, the physical abuse she suffered by the hands of then boyfriend, Chris Brown, is forever etched in the history books. Jennifer Aniston was one of the highest paid television actresses and most envied celebrity wife when she married actor Brad Pitt. However, her seemingly perfect world fell apart in plain view when her husband began a romantic relationship with fellow actress, Angelina Jolie, whom he subsequently married after his divorce from Jennifer. Years later, Angelina filed for divorce, thrusting her and Pitt's relationship issues into the spotlight.

For those who live their lives in the public eye, the hurt is magnified because it is broadcast repeatedly and out in the open for the world to comment. They often have to plaster on a smile or live a façade to maintain their public image. Fortunately, most of us can go through our personal challenges with some privacy, if we choose. The way we go through the experience, is however, a choice.

In 2009, I was diagnosed with polymyositis, an autoimmune disorder which affects the mobility of the limbs due to a weakening of muscle mass. It was extremely difficult for me to walk long distances or to climb stairs. At my weakest point, I struggled to lift my arms, to brush my hair, and needed assistance putting on my clothes. There were some days when I felt angry because my body would not cooperate and perform the way it had once performed. Prior to my diagnosis, I had been able to run up to four miles daily. In a short period of time, my athletic ability was reduced to barely being able to walk. There were moments when I felt sad and wondered how long I would have to take steroids, which treated the polymyositis, but led to weight gain. However, I never thought of allowing my condition to defeat me. In many ways, I accomplished more during the time I was dealing with the illness than I have during healthier periods in my life. Although it was difficult having to deal with a health issue, the lessons I learned from the experience are priceless – much like a diamond.

Abolitionist and writer, Frederick Douglass said, "Without struggle, there is no progress." When you face difficult situations, know it is a part of your journey. I recall an especially difficult point in my life when I felt I was catching it from every angle. In the midst of my pain and frustration, I spoke to other people who were dealing with their own challenges. What I remember most about the conversations is the people were going through the fires. No matter how difficult the circumstance, they refused to be consumed or destroyed.

Although no one looks forward to facing tragedy, heartache, or disappointment, there is good which can be derived from the bad. If you stay focused on how hard a situation seems or how challenging your circumstances are, you will likely feel frustrated, overwhelmed, and discouraged. However, when you decide to shift your focus to the lesson or the solution, your perspective will change. You will begin to see your situation through a different type of lens – one that can withstand even the hottest flame. When you come through it all, you are guaranteed to shine brilliantly, just like a diamond!

BE FIREPROOF REFLECTION

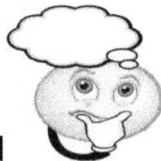

❖ Think about items which are flame resistant and those which are flammable. What allows the flame resistant items to withstand heat unlike the flammable items?

❖ In what ways are you fireproof? In what ways are you flammable?

❖ Reflect on the last five years of your life. Identify some of the struggles you faced. Next to each struggle, think of one way in which you have progressed or advanced as a result of having gone through the struggle.

BE GRATEFUL

"A grateful mindset can set you free from the prison of disempowerment and the shackles of misery."
~Steve Maraboli, Author

Show me an unhappy person and I can tell you he is focused on what he does not have rather than being grateful for what he has been given. It is easy to forget the importance of being grateful when life becomes busy. You can become distracted by your weekly schedule of activities and all you need to accomplish. Maybe work is keeping you busier than usual. Family issues have you feeling emotionally drained. The lack of finances and an abundance of bills can create added pressure and stress. It is during these times when you must slow down and think about all for which you have to be grateful. However, it can be a challenge to feel thankful when the pressure is on and stress levels are high.

There have certainly been times in my life when gratitude took a backseat. During one particular season in life, I was very unhappy at my job. While I wanted to just pick up and leave, I knew it was best to wait for God to open another opportunity. I prayed for God to move me, but nothing happened. Each day, I searched for job openings. I was even open to taking a job in a different field if it would get me out of the job I had at the time. The longer I stayed, the more miserable I felt. Then, I heard a message regarding being thankful and living with gratitude. In the message, the speaker talked about the importance of giving thanks for small things and living with a grateful mindset. After hearing the message, I decided to change my attitude. Rather than focus on everything I hated about my job, I decided to focus on what I enjoyed. Each day, I began the day by speaking positively about my day. I said aloud – "I am thankful for the opportunity to impact the lives of others. Today is going to be a great day. I am going to be effective and productive. This is going to be my best day yet!"

Even when I did not feel it, I spoke those words of positivity out loud. I even made a list of things for which I was grateful and people whom I was thankful to have in my life. Sometimes, we can develop an attitude of expectation over appreciation for the people closest to us. There is a fifty-six year age difference between me and my great-grandmother. She could have easily passed on taking the responsibility to raise me. After all, she was sixty-one and had already raised her children and most of her grandchildren. She could have argued it was her time to rest and enjoy life. However, because she rose to the occasion, I am who I am today. She never missed any activity in which I was involved. She gave me a strong foundation in Christ and modeled a life of loving and giving. I am eternally grateful for the sacrifices she made and try to thank her by enriching her life, as much as possible. Without a doubt, she was number one on the list.

After making a list of gratitude, I had a new attitude. I no longer dreaded going to my job and became more effective and productive in my position. While God did not remove me from the situation, the message I received helped me to change my outlook toward the situation. Not long after I began to give thanks and have a grateful mindset, several key people on my job were transferred. A whole new team was brought in and the entire atmosphere of the workplace changed for the better.

It can be especially difficult to have a grateful mindset when you are going through a challenging time. Your best friend betrays you and you feel hurt, not grateful. You lose your job and you feel discouraged, not thankful. When you face a disappointment, it is natural to wonder why it happened to you and how it fits in the grand scheme of life. Taking a moment to be conscious of the times when it all worked out in your favor can help you view your situation from a different vantage point. It may seem counterintuitive to be grateful for the hardships you face. However, complaining about how bad a situation is never makes the situation better. In fact, complaining and focusing on the wrong things can often lead to negativity and self-pity. One of the best ways to change a negative perspective is to take the time to be thankful.

While in law school, I had a summer internship with the Office of the Public Defender. Contrary to popular opinion, many public defenders work hard to defend their clients. Their job is not easy, as they are given a heavy caseload and often work long hours with no overtime. The elected Public Defender at the time was one of the smartest bosses I've had. He understood the pressure and stress his employees faced and did a great job making his employees feel appreciated. He was not stingy with compliments and took the time to recognize an employee when she was doing her job well, even if the outcome was not the one expected. There was actually a Nerf basketball goal set up in a corner of the office. When staff and employees needed a break, they would go and shoot hoops for a couple of minutes. Someone could question why he would allow such activity in a professional setting. Because he did, however, his employees knew he was aware of the challenges and stress they dealt with daily. No matter who I spoke to in the office, they were all thankful to have him as their boss.

Similarly, if you are in leadership, you can improve your team by showing appreciation. For years, the U.S. Department of Labor reported a lack of appreciation as the number one reason people leave their jobs. Several other polls found more than half of Americans did not receive any recognition in the workplace during the course of a year. However, a number of studies show recognition and appreciation can be great motivators for improving productivity and performance. According to an article in the Harvard Business Review, feeling appreciated generally lifts a person's spirits. When people feel appreciated, they exhibit positive energy which is often contagious to those around them. Likewise, when people do not feel appreciated, they are more likely to complain and display a negative attitude, which can also be contagious.

In the U.S., we celebrate Thanksgiving as a time to focus on gratitude and showing appreciation. How much different would our lives be if we developed an attitude of thanksgiving each week rather than once a year? Saying "thank you" and showing appreciation are valuable gifts which do not cost anything. Amazingly, showing a little appreciation can make a big difference in a person's life.

When I received an award from my job, some of my students decided to surprise me with a pizza party and cake in recognition of the honor. I was quite overwhelmed by their effort. They enlisted the school security and other teachers to get me out of the classroom so they could pull it all off without a hitch. The coup de grace was a video they made thanking me for all

I had done for them. Each student took turns explaining how thankful they were for the time and effort I put into helping them develop and providing exposure and opportunities. Being the tough teacher I was, I didn't make it to the end of the video without the waterworks flowing!

There is something profound about giving thanks and showing gratitude. Unfortunately, people do not express it to one another enough. I heard a story about a wealthy family in which the husband was a famous surgeon and the wife, who once had a thriving career in entertainment, had become primarily a stay at home mom. Since they had a couple of children under five, the mom's days were usually filled with diaper changes, potty breaks, laundry, and play dates. In addition, she was in charge of making most of the decisions for the new luxury home they were having built. One day, she opened up to a friend, sharing how she felt about her situation. She knew her husband loved her, but she was not sure he appreciated all the work and effort she put into their family and household. She was not asking him to buy her a new diamond bracelet or an expensive bag. All she wanted was for him to acknowledge her effort and say thank you.

A genuine "thank you" takes little time to say and can mean so much to the receiving party. Yet, the words often remain unsaid. A sincere pat on the back may be just the encouragement a person needs to finish the day strong. If you are in a relationship, make sure you are not taking the person you are in relationship with for granted. If you have a friend who has been loyal and dependable, you should let her know what she means to you. You should not wait for a special occasion to thank her for being a great friend. If you have a co-worker who has assisted you or a neighbor who has been good to you, let him know how much you appreciate it. A little appreciation **goes a long way**.

During the holidays, we experienced one of the most frightening nights of our lives. We thought our beloved dog, Coco, was missing. My husband and I felt helpless. We were stuck in evening traffic a few miles away from our home. It was getting dark, and we were extremely worried. In a panic, I called my neighbor and asked if she could walk our subdivision to look for our dog. Without any hesitation, she and her daughter walked our neighborhood calling our dog's name. Fortunately, we discovered Coco had been hiding in the house the entire time. However, I was incredibly grateful for my neighbor's willingness to help our family in a time of need. I later called to express my gratitude and gave her a gift card to show how much I appreciated her being such a great neighbor.

Gratitude can be expressed and experienced in many different ways. Make sure you are living a life of gratitude. Think of ways you can show appreciation for those in your life or people over whom you may have influence. Don't be surprised if one small act of appreciation makes a big difference!

BE GRATEFUL REFLECTION

❖ Think about the most memorable way someone expressed gratitude in your life. How did it make you feel? What can you do to make someone else feel the same?

❖ When was the last time you expressed sincere gratitude? How was it received?

❖ Think of a time when you failed to show appreciation. If you could show it now, what would you say or do?

BE HEALTHY

"Nothing tastes as good as being healthy feels."
~Author Unknown

Fried mozzarella sticks. Buffalo wings. Pizza with extra cheese. Potato skins, fries, mashed potatoes – any type of potato! Oh, how I love potatoes! These were some of my favorite foods before I knew what I now know. After having Tristan, it was challenging to lose the baby weight. Because I was breastfeeding, I began to look for ways to make healthy food choices. In an effort to squeeze in more vegetables, I started making green shakes in the morning, which included leafy greens, Greek yogurt, fruit, and flax seed. I chose leaner cuts of meat, whenever possible, and began to monitor my sugar intake.

My friend, a registered dietician, told me to eat my calories rather than drink them. Gradually, I began to cut back on the amount of juice and soda I drank. Did you know the average 12 ounce can of soda has 44 grams of sugar? Many people drink more than 12 ounces because they consume multiple sodas a day or drink a larger serving at one time. 44 grams of sugar is equivalent to 11 teaspoons of sugar. I wouldn't dare put 11 teaspoons of sugar in a 12 ounce drink. Once I knew how much sugar was in a 12 ounce can, soda became less appealing. The more I began to make healthier food choices, the less I wanted to binge on the unhealthy foods. Although I definitely still enjoy a cheeseburger, fries, and soda, I am selective about how often I allow myself to indulge.

Being healthy is not about being skinny or achieving a certain dress size. Healthy living is a lifestyle decision. It is important to consult your doctor and be realistic about your health goals. I know people who refuse to go to the doctor, but seeing a healthcare professional is an important part of maintaining your health. It is better to practice preventive care and implement positive choices in your lifestyle before you are made to do it as the result of a medical diagnosis. Don't wait until you are diagnosed with diabetes or high blood pressure to decide it's time to lose weight or make healthier food selections. Your body is like a fine automobile. If you treat it right and get regular maintenance, it will run well for a long time. However, if you ignore it, your body is sure to shut down.

If you want to achieve your goals, it is imperative to make your physical and mental health a priority. Pursuing your goals can take an enormous amount of energy and stamina. According to the Center for Disease Control (CDC), in 2016, over sixty percent of Americans were overweight or obese. Additionally, the CDC reported an estimated nine million American children and teens suffered from issues related to obesity or being overweight. Your health goals are personal and specific to what is important in your life. There is no cookie cutter design for being healthy. Although what works for one person, may not work for you, there are common denominators which can help anyone develop a healthier lifestyle.

I consider myself somewhat of a foodie, but it is hard to ignore the benefits of healthy eating once your body has become accustomed to it. Four to five mornings a week, I make a green shake to get a jump start on my vegetable intake. Additionally, I make egg muffins, to which I typically add shrimp, spinach, mushroom, and a little cheese. They are much like omelets, except they are baked in a muffin pan. I usually take my lunch to work, which generally consists of leftovers from the night before. For dinner, I typically bake a lean cut of meat and try to have at least two vegetables and one starch. Eating healthy can be time consuming and costly, but it is worth the effort.

On average, I follow an 80/20 rule. Eighty percent of the time, I am cognizant of what I eat and make an effort to eat healthy. Although I do not count calories, I take notice of foods high in calories and sugar. For example, if I have a donut in the morning, I make sure I balance it with a healthy lunch and dinner. For me, it is better to eat the one donut and enjoy it rather than deprive myself of it altogether. I am more likely to eat several donuts if I try to deny myself of sweets completely. The diet industry makes several billion dollars each year from the popularity of fad diets and trends. However, many people find it challenging to keep up with the demands of such diets because they are highly restrictive or offer quick results with little sustainability. Eating and exercising in moderation has allowed me to develop a healthy lifestyle.

If you are not moving each day, you should be. The more you move, the more energy you have. Sitting around actually makes you feel more tired and can definitely make getting active more difficult. If you do not like exercising at the gym or having a formal routine, find creative ways to get yourself moving. You can do yardwork or housework as a way of being active. During the summer months, I often speed walk the malls because it is too hot outside for me to go running. If you are physically able to do it, take the stairs instead of the elevator. If you are really motivated, sign up for a class.

It can be incredibly inspiring when you exercise with a group.

There are periods in my life when my workout routine is more consistent than others. However, if I go too long without exercising, I become irritable and can feel my body began to get tense. It's as if my body is craving the workout. While I enjoy the benefits of exercising, my schedule will not allow me to go to the gym daily. To supplement my workout routine, I wear a step tracker and try to log a minimum of 12,000 steps daily. Sometimes, I get up to 20,000 steps! On those days, I don't need to workout ☺

Scientific studies show sleep is also essential to your overall health. Sleep is necessary for the healing of your heart and blood vessels. According to several studies, chronic sleep deprivation can be linked to an increase in health issues, such as heart disease, high blood pressure, and stroke. Getting adequate sleep has been said to boost creativity, alertness, and increase productivity. Before being diagnosed with polymyositis, I routinely overbooked and over-extended myself, which is why I confused the symptoms of the disorder with being tired from my work schedule. Because I am task-oriented, I would plough right through whatever I needed to finish, even if it meant working ten or twelve hours without stopping for lunch. However, I have since learned working without taking a break only hurts my body and overall health. Sleep and rest are necessary to help restore your body from the wear and tear it endures daily. When you fail to get adequate rest, you can become cranky, impatient, and physically ill. You cannot live an empowered life if you are too tired to be your best self.

While physical health is important, mental and emotional health are equally as significant. In an effort to take care of my mental and emotional health, I read books, attend conferences, seek professional therapy, and share with my inner circle. People often feel they can manage their emotions by pretending they don't exist or burying them deep within. However, unresolved emotions often manifest into destructive behaviors. Having a safe environment in which you can express your dreams, fears, goals, needs, and concerns is important to your mental and emotional well-being. You need to surround yourself with people who have your best interest in mind and provide positive support.

Similarly, your spiritual wellness is also important. Regardless of your belief system, it is necessary to have an outlet. Nurturing your spiritual and emotional health is a way to attain tranquility and peace in life. Being aware of your core values and beliefs is paramount in your decision-making. Understanding what you view as right or wrong will often determine what you set as a high priority in your life. Your spiritual wellness is also related to how you view people and the world around you. Discovering a purpose in life and reflecting on how your life experiences have influenced you can provide you with a sense of direction for your future. You can attend to your spiritual health by engaging in religious or faith based practices, praying, meditating, reading or studying faith based text, reciting affirmations, journaling, practicing yoga, or retreating to a place you designate as your quiet spot. The key is not to ignore the importance of your spiritual health because it will guide your emotions.

Much like we attend professional development and training for our careers, we need to maintain our physical health and engage in personal development for personal growth. Not long ago, I had a conversation with an acquaintance that was facing some personal challenges. During the conversation, I suggested she seek professional therapy as an option to help her deal with the issues. Her response was, "Really? I didn't think I needed therapy. I didn't think it was that bad."

The perfect opportunity to make it better is when it isn't that bad. Unfortunately, people often wait until a situation is almost irreparable to seek help. Being healthy is one of the greatest gifts you can give yourself and your family. I've never known someone to invest in his physical, mental, or emotional well-being and regret the investment. Taking the risk to be healthy and invest in yourself is one investment which is sure to bring a great return.

BE HEALTHY REFLECTION

❖ Based on a scale of 1 to 10, with 1 being the lowest and 10 being the highest, how would you rate your physical, emotional, and spiritual health? Give an explanation for each rating.

❖ In which area(s) do you need the most improvement? What is one step you can take to improve in the area(s)?

❖ Identify the obstacles which potentially keep you from improving in the area(s). What will you do to overcome the obstacles?

BE INTENTIONAL

"Every morning in Africa, a gazelle wakes up, it knows it must outrun the fastest lion or it will be killed. Every morning in Africa, a lion wakes up. It knows it must run faster than the slowest gazelle, or it will starve. It doesn't matter whether you're the lion or a gazelle. When the sun comes up, you'd better be running."
~African Proverb

Jill Right and Jack Wrong worked in sales for the same company. Working on commission, they were often in competition with each other for profitable clients. Jill was very intentional about how she planned each day. She made a point to begin each day by declaring, "This is going to be the best day. I have yet to make my biggest sale. I know good things are going to happen to me." Jill was also very organized and kept her client information in an online database she could access using any mobile device. If a client had a question, Jill was able to access important information and any previous sales she had made within seconds. Before leaving work, Jill usually made a to-do list of the tasks she needed to complete the next day.

Jack, however, was not as focused. He hated being in competition with Jill and often told her, "I don't know why I even try. You're so much better than me. All the good clients go to you, anyway." Additionally, Jack was much less organized. He usually scribbled information on a sticky note here or a folder there, promising himself he would organize his lists one day. Because Jack was distrustful of technology, he refused to upgrade his sales information to an electronic device.

Instead, he used a binder, which was often stuffed with papers flowing from top to bottom.

Last Monday, Jack met with a high profile client who would net him a large commission. On Wednesday morning, the client called Jack and requested he email the client a copy of an important document they worked on during their meeting. Unfortunately, Jack had tossed the document in his notebook of papers and misplaced it. When Jack informed the client the document was missing, the client promptly requested to be assigned to Jill. Jack was reprimanded by his supervisor and placed on probation. Not only did Jack lose an important client, but he also lost an opportunity to be taken seriously in his profession.

Being intentional with your words and actions can have a great impact on how you see yourself. Imagine if you walked around proclaiming, "Nothing good ever happens to me. If it's not one thing, it's another. I'll probably never get out of my situation." If you walk around speaking those negative words to yourself, you will stay right in the situation you are in. It is difficult to achieve greatness in life without being purposeful in your actions. If you expect the worst to happen and welcome it into your life through your thoughts, words, and actions, the worst will take a front row seat. Your lack of good breaks or opportunities may be attributed to your focus. Much like Jill Right and Jack Wrong, you have the ability to determine your reality. What you believe about yourself inevitably shows up in your choices.

If you speak and believe you will be a millionaire, you will also likely take the steps needed to make it happen in your life. Likewise, if you believe your situation will never change, you are not likely to take the steps to make a change. I believe in the principle of calling things which are not as if they already are. As a result, I intentionally speak about the goals I want to accomplish as if they have already been set in motion. It is not *if* I become a best-selling author, but rather *when*.

What you say has more impact in your life than what anyone says about you or to you. You have the power to influence your destiny with the words you speak over your life. If you say you are undisciplined, then you will likely behave in an undisciplined way. If you say you always make the wrong decisions, chances are you will find yourself making poor decisions. If your self-talk is negative, you can expect to have negative results. Have you ever heard a champion calling himself a loser? Absolutely not! Winners think, speak, and act like winners.   Winners understand the power of being intentional with their thoughts, words, and actions, which is why you will hear them encouraging themselves when they have an obstacle to overcome. *You can do it! You've got this! Stay focused on the goal!* These are some of the affirmations you might hear in a winner's circle.

While words alone may not limit your opportunities and potential, the effect the words have on you will. When I am exercising, it is important for me to engage in positive self-talk. During every workout, there is a point when I would like to stop. Sometimes, I am just not in the mood and I rely on self-motivation to get me through the routine. I tell myself, *You are more than halfway finished. You've come too far to give up now. Your legs are strong and powerful. This is nothing to you!* Even if I don't feel it at the time, those words encourage me enough to complete my routine. What if I said the opposite? *You should just quit. You're tired. You might as well stop and have a donut.* I am sure those negative words would have the same influence, but with a different outcome. Choosing your words carefully and purposefully can help you stay focused on what is important to you.

You should also seek to be intentional with your gift. When I read *The Purpose Driven Life* by Rick Warren, it had a lasting impression on my life. It was life changing for me because it challenged me to identify my passion. In doing so, I discovered my purpose in life. Although many people fear standing in front of an audience and giving a presentation, I am excited when given the opportunity. As a child, I often spoke in church, giving the welcome for special events or reciting a lengthy speech for Easter or Christmas. Throughout high school, I further developed my public speaking skills by entering speech contests.

For as long as I can remember, I have enjoyed speaking and writing. As I stated earlier, I started writing my first book when I was in the fourth grade. As an undergraduate in college, I majored in English Creative Writing. While many of my friends struggled to write their papers, I actually enjoyed it. Over the years, I discovered I not only had an interest in speaking and writing, but I had a gift for it. As I read *The Purpose Driven Life*, I realized I can use my gift to influence the lives of other people, hence discovering my purpose in life. When you understand the reason why you are here, it is nearly impossible to live life without being intentional.

When you wake up in the morning, you are granted a new twenty four hours to make a difference in someone's life, to make your mark on the world, and to leave a legacy. Therefore, it is imperative to be intentional with your time. If you have not set any goals, do not have a plan, and are not taking any steps forward, you are wasting time. You should approach each day with a purpose because your approach can make a tremendous difference in your results at the end of the day. My grandmother used to say, "The early bird gets the worm." Since I was not a morning person, I would respond, "I don't like worms!" However, I have learned while you are sleeping until noon, business deals are being negotiated, degrees are being earned, interviews are taking place, and decisions are being made. If you are not in the right place at the right time, you may miss an opportunity.

The lion and the eagle are two exceptional creatures from which we can learn lessons about intentionality. Interestingly, lions travel in a selective group known as a pride. Although female cubs remain with one another for life, male cubs do not. When males reach the age of maturity, the dominant male of the pride will kick out the male cubs because he views them as a threat to his position. Young males then go out in search of a pride for which they can become the dominant male. When a young male challenges an older lion and wins, one of his first priorities is to kill off any offspring of the previous male. He then begins to mate with the lionesses to establish his own legacy.

Although it might seem brutal, lions are intentional about whom they allow in their clique. They intentionally surround themselves with those whom are loyal. The dominant male only wants lions in the pride that will work together and support the goals or objectives of the pride. Furthermore, when a lion hunts his prey, he often lies patiently awaiting the right time to make his move. Lions are very strategic, as most of their prey are faster and can outrun them. As a result, the lion must be intentional about when to strike. Much like the lion, you should be intentional with the steps you take and the decisions you make.

Similarly, eagles are selective about the company they keep. You will never see an eagle running around with chickens because eagles understand they are not like other birds. While other birds must flap their wings, eagles soar above the clouds without flapping. They spread out their wing span and glide through the air using the thermal winds. When an eagle is threatened by a pest, the eagle simply flies to an altitude the pest cannot achieve. In the same way, there will be times you may have to intentionally separate yourself from others to reach the level you were intended to achieve.

Be purposeful in your speech and strategic in your actions. Choose to start each day with a plan and account for how you spend your time. If you are intentional with your words, your gifts, and your time, you will soar to great heights, just like the eagle!

BE INTENTIONAL REFLECTION

❖ What words or phrases do you need to intentionally add to your self-talk? What words or phrases do you need to eliminate from your self-talk?

❖ Consider how you can be more intentional with your time. For the next week, make a to-do list of the tasks you need to complete (work, home, leisure). At the end of each day, evaluate how effective you were at eliminating the tasks from your list. Identify any points where you wasted time or did not manage time effectively.

❖ Identify at least one area in which you excel. How do you use your talent or gift intentionally? What can you do to use your talent or gift in a more purposeful way?

BE JOYFUL

"A joyful spirit is evidence of a grateful heart."
~Maya Angelou, Author and Poet

Vanessa was a high school magnet teacher with a demanding schedule. While she taught classes, she was also responsible for coordinating field trips, recruiting prospective students, and managing community partnerships. As part of her duties, she often visited middle schools to give presentations about the programs offered at her school. One Wednesday, in particular, Vanessa was especially busy. She was tied up in unexpected meetings for most of the morning and was scheduled to give a presentation at a neighboring middle school in the afternoon.

When she arrived at the middle school, the vice principal seemed surprised to see her. He had forgotten Vanessa was scheduled to visit and had not made any arrangements for her presentation. While the school personnel attempted to round up students to attend the presentation, Vanessa began to setup the materials. As she began to rifle through her recruitment bag, she discovered she was missing some of her marketing materials, including her table skirt and banner. Rather than get upset, Vanessa adapted and gave a revised version of her presentation. When it was over, she smiled to herself and laughed. What a day it had been!

Traffic jam in the morning. An unexpected emergency. A computer issue causes a delay. Inevitably, you will be faced with circumstances beyond your control. It is better to have a lighthearted attitude than to be constantly stressed when things do not go the way you planned. Unless it is life threatening or life changing, you should be willing to find the humor in most any situation. Laughter is good for the soul and can take the stress out of most any situation. In Vanessa's case, her day could have been completely ruined if she had allowed those unexpected events to sour her attitude. Instead, she chose to not only laugh at the situation, but at herself. Sometimes you need to lighten up and let yourself off the hook.

Of course, there are issues in life which are serious and should not be taken lightly. Certainly, you should not blow off your responsibilities or make light of issues which deserve your thoughtful attention. However, most of your day-to-day activities will be routine. It can be easy to get stressed out because traffic is moving slowly or your computer crashed. Maybe you lost your keys and now you are going to be late to wherever you needed to be first thing in the morning. It will not do you any good to get sour or start complaining about your circumstances. If you maintain a jovial spirit and refuse to let minor issues spoil your day, you will be back on track in no time.

Do you know people who are too uptight? If they make one mistake, it ruins their mood. They may not know it, but they probably are not a lot of fun to be around. Others have to tip toe around their feelings and constantly worry if they are going to be set off by the smallest inconvenience. Life is too unpredictable to allow every mishap or annoyance to put you in a bad mood. When you go through difficult times, it is okay to vent your frustrations. If you face a loss, you need to give yourself time to grieve in order to heal. However, you should not allow venting and grieving to become a constant in your life. Even after the most devastating loss, you must find a way to experience joy and get your smile back.

In Proverbs 17:22, the scripture says "a cheerful heart is good medicine, but a broken spirit dries up the bones." In essence, laughter is good for the mind, body, and soul. Whenever I am feeling down or upset about a problem, I look for a funny movie or seek out a friend with whom I can share a laugh. Sometimes, I laugh so hard, my side hurts and tears stream down my face. That is good medicine!

You may feel as though you have few reasons to smile or laugh. Maybe life has dealt you some tough blows and you have a hard time finding the humor in any situation. No matter what you are going through, you have something for which you can be grateful. If you are reading this book, you woke up on this side of the ground. You can be happy you are alive. Your situation may not be what you want it to be, but you have the power to turn it around. It all begins with the right attitude and a smile.

There has been extensive research done on the positive effects of laughter. Various medical and psychological studies show laughter can benefit your overall physical health, mental well-being, and social interactions. Medical research shows laughter triggers the release of endorphins in your body, often referred to as the natural feel good chemical. This is why you feel so good, almost like you are floating on a cloud, after a really good laugh. Have you ever witnessed someone smiling long after the laughter has stopped? It's those endorphins being released!

Additionally, other studies have linked laughter to boosting the immune system, aiding in the prevention of heart disease, and being used as supportive therapy for cancer treatment. A good laugh can also be contagious.

Whenever you see others laughing and having a good time, it is hard not to want to be in on the fun, as well. Having a good sense of humor not only helps to relieve stress and improve your mood, but it can also help you to bond with others and improve your relationships.

When you make an effort to live in joy and peace, life is enjoyable. While you cannot choose the outcome of each situation, you can choose how you will come out of it. You can be the person whom everyone has to tip toe around; or, you can be the one who brings light into a dark situation. Sometimes just a smile can create a different atmosphere. Remember, smiles are free and are often reciprocated.

I recently read a book to my son about a grumpy lobster. In the story, the lobster was grumpy for no apparent reason other than he found fault with the world around him. He complained about the food he had to eat. When it was time to play with his friends, he complained about the games they wanted to play. Nothing satisfied the lobster. Finally, his friends grew tired of his complaints and decided they didn't want to hang out with him anymore. Their decision forced the lobster to evaluate his attitude. When he saw his friends laughing and enjoying life without him, he realized he didn't want to be the grumpy lobster anymore. He wanted to live a more enjoyable life filled with smiles and laughter. He made a conscious decision to change his attitude and he replaced his frowns and complaints with smiles and gratitude.

I love to be around people who make me laugh, which really isn't hard to do because I genuinely want to laugh. My great-grandmother is one of the most joyful people I know. She is always laughing, mostly at herself. She doesn't take herself too seriously. If she mispronounces a word, she laughs it off and tries to pronounce it correctly. If she forgets to do something or makes a mistake, she doesn't get flustered. She finds humor in whatever she does and it makes her a joy to be around. She can be serious when the time calls for her to be serious. Most of the time, however, she is smiling or trying to put a smile on someone else's face. I am convinced her positive attitude and cheerful outlook on life have helped her to remain healthy and live the long life she has lived.

Similarly, I try to find joy and humor in my daily activities, such as walking my dog and hanging out with my son. When I pay close attention, my dog will usually do something which makes me smile or laugh. Each day, without fail, Tristan says something which I find hilarious. As a four-year-old, he is not trying to be funny – he just is. One weekend, I cleaned out my walk-in closet, so I could actually walk into it. It was a disaster area! I had pulled everything out of the closet so I could toss the items I no longer needed and rearrange what I was going to keep. There was so much stuff, I couldn't maneuver around in the bathroom, which leads to the closet.

My son walked in and exclaimed, "Mommy! What are you doing? You made a BIG mess! I'm telling Daddy! I burst into laughter for several reasons. First, the truthfulness of the situation was funny because I had made a big mess. Second, the idea of him telling on me was funny. For goodness sake, I'm his mommy! More than anything, I found humor in his tone and him reprimanding me as I do him when he has made a big mess in his room. The next morning, he woke up, took a look at my now accessible walk-in closet and said approvingly, "Good job, mommy. Good job!"

Life can get heavy, but it doesn't have to weigh you down. Whether it's a conversation with your funniest girlfriend, watching your favorite television comedy, or spending time with the people who make you smile, choose to have a joyful spirit. Don't spend time sweating the small stuff. Each day, take a large dose of good medicine and keep a smile on your face!

BE JOYFUL REFLECTION

❖ For the next three days, keep a journal of how you feel when you wake up in the morning and before you go to sleep at night. During the day, track the number of times you smile and laugh throughout the day. At the end of the three days, evaluate how you think smiling and laughter relate to your mood.

❖ Who and/or what makes you smile most? What about the person and/or thing makes you feel cheerful?

❖ How can you incorporate more humor into your life? What can you do with family or friends to engage in laughter?

BE KIND

"Be the type of person you want to meet."
~Author Unknown

The parable of the Good Samaritan is about a Jewish man who was jumped and beaten by a group of men while traveling. He was stripped of his clothes, robbed, and left for dead on the side of the road. Shortly after the man was beaten, a priest came along traveling the same path. As a priest, he should have been ready and willing to assist the man in need. Rather than help, however, the priest crossed to the other side of the road and pretended not to see the man needing assistance.

Later, a Levite, whose job was to assist priests with their work, walked down the same path. Although he could clearly see the man was beaten, badly bruised, and in need of help, the Levite did not stop. A few minutes later, a Samaritan man walked down the path. It is important to note the Samaritans did not like Jewish people. During this period in history, Jewish people did not treat Samaritans very well. As a result, the two groups did not get along.

Given the history between the two groups, it would not have been surprising if the Samaritan had kept walking like the men before him. However, he was different. Instead of ignoring the man in need, the Samaritan stopped and showed compassion. He poured expensive oil and wine on the man's sores to keep them from getting worse. Then, he put bandages on the man and placed him on a donkey to transport him to a place where he would be safe. Once they reached the destination, the Samaritan paid for the man to stay there until he was well.

Surely, the Samaritan in the story had somewhere else to be or something else to do besides caring for a stranger who was actually an enemy. However, he made a conscious decision to put someone else before himself and show kindness. The other two men missed an opportunity to do good because they were too focused on themselves.

One day, I observed one of my co-workers struggling to carry supplies to her classroom. I was on my way to run an errand and had a million and one things on my to-do list. I was focused on accomplishing my goal, but when I saw her, something in my spirit told me to offer help. I met her at the foot of the stairs, grabbed half of her belongings, and headed to her classroom. It only took me a few minutes and was a minor detour from my plans. But, it was a great help to my co-worker.

It is easier to be kind when you are not busy, when things are going great in your personal life, or to people who are nice and kind to you. It is much harder to show kindness when you have a deadline to meet and you are under pressure. It can be difficult to be nice to the person who has offended you, hurt you, insulted you, or mistreated you. Yet, the people who need to receive your kindness most may be the very ones who have not been so kind to you. I have often heard people who are hurting tend to hurt others. Regardless of your situation, you can make a choice to be good to others. In most instances, a kind act takes little effort from you, but can make a world of difference to the person on the receiving end.

Have you ever stood in line at the grocery store next to someone who complained about the wait and the slow cashier? How many times have you been in a restaurant and watched a mother try to wrangle her kids from climbing the walls? When was the last time someone in a car behind you blew his horn before the traffic light turned green?

One way you can show kindness is by being polite. I was taught to say *Yes ma'am, Please, Thank you,* and *No sir.* While some people might find it old fashioned, being polite never goes out of style. As a girl scout, my troop leader gave awards at the end of the year. I'll never forget receiving an award because I had manners and was always polite. In a society where people want everything quick, fast, and in a hurry, there is little time to be kind. Although most people are taught to be polite and courteous at an early age, the practice of being kind is often forgotten as we go through our daily activities. In passing, you may ask people, "How are you?" However, it can be easy to move on before you receive the answer and show little genuine concern for how the other person is actually feeling. It has become common place to say, "Have a nice day!" Yet, how many of us really mean it when we say it?

Before I married my husband, my routine was to stay late after work on Fridays. Although my husband and I were dating at the time, we were in a long distance relationship. When most of my colleagues were rushing to get home and start the weekend, I used those Friday evenings to catch up on my work. Usually, the custodians and I were the only employees left in the building. As a result, I got to know the custodians quite well. Each Friday night, without me ever asking, one of the custodians would take the time to walk me to my car. While I had finished my day, their shift was just beginning. I am sure they had a long list of tasks to complete. Certainly, walking me to the other side of the building was not part of their job duty and could have been viewed as an interruption to their work schedule.

However, without fail, they collectively made sure I arrived at my car safely each Friday night. Their acts of kindness left an indelible mark.

Most of us engage in service in some capacity of our lives. Whether you are a teacher serving students, a waitress serving patrons, an usher at a faith-based institution, or the CEO of a major corporation, you likely provide a service. Consider the manner in which you provide your service. Do you greet people with a smile? Are you pleasant to be around? If someone is in need, would she feel comfortable asking for your help? When was the last time you inconvenienced yourself to assist someone else with no expectation of anything in return. Your answers to those questions will reveal a lot about the level of kindness you show to others.

Think about the people who serve you. Are you courteous in the manner you greet your waiter at the restaurant? What tone do you use when you ask for help in the grocery store? Are you friendly to the person who cleans your office? How do you treat the guy installing the cable or painting your home? The Golden Rule, "Do unto others as you would have them do unto you" applies to all areas of your life. It is natural to be concerned about yourself and focused on your own personal needs and desires. However, you have to consciously make an effort to concern yourself with the needs of others. If you want to know how to treat someone else, just consider how you want to be treated.

Giving compliments is another easy way you can show kindness. A positive word about someone else costs you nothing, but can mean the world to the person receiving the compliment. There are some people who have never been told they are beautiful, smart, or talented. You may be the only one to deposit those seeds of greatness. If you see another woman with a nice haircut or a pretty dress, tell her. Don't keep it to yourself. You are not doing any good to keep those positive thoughts inside. People need to hear words of kindness spoken over them. You never know how your words might impact someone else.

When I first began teaching, I received a kind gift from one of my students. He made me a certificate honoring me as his nicest teacher. He told me how much he looked forward to me saying – "Good morning class!" He observed whether the class had behaved well or poorly, I greeted them positively each day. His certificate is probably one of the more important honors I have ever received. It is a reminder to me that there are people who need to see a smile or hear kind words. Whenever you have the chance, take advantage of the opportunity to speak positivity and kindness over those with whom you come in contact.

In most cases, the acts of kindness you show will require very little of you but can mean a great deal to someone else. It easy to be kind to the people you love and with whom you share close relationship. However, it is important to also show kindness to those you do not know, like the story of the Good Samaritan. Look for ways to be kind to others, whether it is an unexpected good deed, a sincere compliment, or a genuine smile. Your ability to show kindness is a valuable and unlimited resource!

BE KIND REFLECTION

❖ What was the last selfless deed you did for someone else? What was the reaction from the person on the receiving end? How did you feel after completing the deed?

❖ What is the nicest thing someone has done for you? How did it make you feel?

❖ For the next 30 days, commit to do at least one kind act per day. Your act of kindness may be as simple as giving a compliment or as unexpected as paying for someone's meal. Keep a journal of your acts of kindness, the responses you receive, and how you feel at the end of each day.

BE LIMITLESS

"You have unlimited talent, unlimited opportunities, and unlimited potential. Live life unlimited!"
~Asiah Wolfolk-Manning, Esq., Author and Speaker

When I was in elementary school, I adored the rap group, Salt-n-Pepa. From their lyrics, to their hairstyles, to their swag, they were everything to me. As a result, I wanted to be a rapper from the time I was old enough to memorize their songs until about eighth grade. I imitated their dance moves and recited their lyrics like I was the fourth member of the group. I had thick gold chains with big medallions and even began writing my own raps. While my original rap songs were not very impressive, it did not deter me from wanting to be a rapper. Once I went to junior high, my focus shifted. I realized I had an interest in psychology and criminology. I enjoyed solving problems, especially figuring out mysteries. By the time I reached high school, I knew I wanted to be a lawyer. Although I did not know any lawyers personally, I had an interest in the way the law worked and a natural gift for speaking.

After high school, I went to college and eventually became a lawyer. However, after practicing law for a short period of time, I decided to pursue other interests. Much of my professional experience has been in education, at the secondary and post-secondary levels. In between, I have pursued my true passion as an author and a speaker. I share none of this with you to be boastful or braggadocios, but rather to encourage you to remove any limitations you or anyone else has placed on you. Live life unlimited!

When a child enters kindergarten, he will inevitably be asked what he wants to be when he grows up. Most children will answer with a career choice they have heard or been exposed to through school or their home life. *I want to be a doctor! I'm going to be a lawyer! I want to be an actress!* When I ask my child what he wants to be when he grows up, I hope he says, "Whatever I can imagine!" While it is important to encourage creativity and nurture goal setting, even at a young age, a child's perception can be influenced by the person asking the question. If the adult asking the question has a limited mindset, there is a good chance he will pass the limited mindset on to the child.

I heard Steve Harvey share a similar personal story. When he was in grade school, his teacher asked him what he wanted to be and his response was a comedian. The teacher, likely meaning no harm, told him he was not being practical. The teacher went on to ask Steve if he knew any comedians. When he replied, "No," the teacher told him to go back and think of a real career to pursue. In essence, the teacher was telling him he could not accomplish his dream. He had a desire to become a comedian. It is evident he had the desire because he was able to communicate it to his teacher, even at a young age. Whether the desire changed should have been left up to Steve. Although he did not know anyone personally making a living as a comedian, he believed it was an option for him. However, the teacher imposed her own limited mindset on a child whose thinking was clearly limitless. Fortunately, he never quit believing he could become a comedian or anything else he could imagine.

There will always be people who try to put you in their box. If you have an idea different from the norm, it will make some people uncomfortable. If your goals are above average, there will always be people who doubt you. Do yourself a favor and tune them out. Everyone does not have to agree with you for you to accomplish your goals. You do not need the approval of everyone around you to move forward with the dreams and desires of your heart. You cannot be afraid to think outside of the box, live outside of the box, or toss the box altogether, if necessary.

Usually, the people who try to put limits on you are restricted by their own limited outlook. It is possible no one in their lives encouraged them to take the limits off. As a result, they cannot see beyond what is exactly in front of them. Unfortunately, limited thinking may be expressed through negativity, criticism, discouraging remarks, and insults.

When my husband was in elementary school, he was playful and rambunctious, like most boys at that age. During class, his third grade teacher made a comment he never forgot. She told him he was never going to be anything. Inconceivably, she felt she had a right to label him and negatively predict his future at eight years old. Growing up in a small town, he often saw his third grade teacher long after he'd passed her class. When she saw him, she would speak, no doubt oblivious to the negative words she had spoken over his life. However, he never forgot the limits she tried to place on him. Fortunately, he did not allow her words to dictate his future. Instead, he used them as motivation to be successful.

No one has the right to tell you what you can or cannot accomplish. It is up to you to determine it for yourself. Sometimes the people who are supposed to encourage or uplift you can be the very ones to who stifle your dreams. There was a great example of this concept in the movie, *The Pursuit of Happyness*. The movie was based on Chris Gardner, a single father, who faced many obstacles while trying to provide a good life for his son. In the movie, Gardner takes his son to the basketball court to shoot hoops. While shooting baskets, Gardner tells his son he should not spend all his time on the court because he will probably be an average player. Gardner explains to his son he was an average player and, as a result, the son will likely also be an average player. Immediately, you can see hope leave the child's face, and he decides he's no longer interested in shooting hoops. When Gardner realizes the impact of passing his limited thinking on to his son, he quickly addresses it. Gardner tells his son not to allow anyone, including his own father, to place limits on what he can do in life. It is a thoughtful moment the father and son share and a profound life lesson.

If someone tries to tell you the goals you have set are too high, stop sharing your goals with him. The person who tries to dissuade you from accomplishing the dreams you have in your heart does not share your unlimited vision. You cannot share your goals and aspirations with everyone because every person is not equipped to understand. There are some people who will only live life by what they can see, feel, and touch. If it is not directly in front of them, it does not exist. However, you do not have to be limited by what others think or believe.

When author, J.K. Rowling, sent out her manuscript for *Harry Potter,* she received over ten rejection letters. She was even told there was very little opportunity to make money as a children's author. It is a good thing she did not listen to the naysayers! She not only found success with her Harry Potter books, but also holds the title as the world's first billionaire author. J.K. Rowling is a barrier breaker, much like Jesse Owens. When he competed in the 1936 Berlin Olympic Games, Jesse Owens broke two Olympic records and won four gold medals. I can imagine many of his peers thought he and the other African-American athletes were crazy to even want to compete in the Olympic Games given Adolf Hitler's beliefs and ideology regarding white supremacy. However, Owens would not be limited by what Hitler or anyone else thought of his ability. His Olympic record for the world broad jump lasted almost twenty-five years. Because he refused to be limited by what was in front of him, Owens made history and established a long-lasting legacy.

The glass ceiling is considered an unofficial barrier to advancement and promotion in a profession. It is a restriction on how high you can go in terms of your position or achievement. Unfortunately, it primarily affects minorities and women. When Hillary Clinton lost the 2016 presidential election, some people referenced the glass ceiling, stating she had gone as far as a woman could go when she served as Secretary of State. While she may not have become the 45th President of the United States, Hilary Clinton helped blow the roof off the glass ceiling. She not only became the first woman nominated by a major political party for the U.S. presidency, but she also won the popular vote in the election. She and many other women before her, like Shirley Chisolm, have paved the way for the future first female U.S. president.

What are the desires of your heart? What do you aspire to do in life? What impact do you expect to have on the world? Whatever you plan to do, make sure you are not restricted by what someone else thinks or believes is possible. If I had waited to know an attorney before becoming one, I might not have a law degree. If I had waited to know a published author before deciding to write, I might not be the author of four books. If you don't know anyone who is doing what you want to do, make a decision to be the first. Anything you can imagine is possible!

BE LIMITLESS REFLECTION

❖ Think about how you view life. In what ways do you think outside the box? In what ways are you willing to live outside the box?

❖ Consider people who are currently doing what you would like to do. What traits or characteristics do they possess? What can you learn from the people you identified?

❖ Who are the people in your life that will support you accomplishing your goals? How can they help you leverage your gifts?

BE MULTIFACETED

"There's more to life than success, and if you can try to
be more well-rounded, you'll be able to enjoy your
success more. It won't own you or control you."
~Ricky Williams, Former Pro NFL Player

My great, great, great grandmother, Bertha Barnes
Smith Dean, was born in the mid to late 1800s in
Marianna, Florida. Although she only had a formal third
grade education, she was well read and extremely
articulate. She worked as a homemaker, washing and
ironing clothes for white families. During a time of blatant
racial inequality, Grandma Bertha owned almost four
acres of land and grew her own peas, green beans, white
potatoes, sweet potatoes, and corn. She played the
piano for the church and was active in the missions
group. Additionally, she was socially active in various
women's organizations in the community. Grandma
Bertha was an eloquent speaker, a talented seamstress,
and an amazing cook. In addition to raising her own three
children, she raised six of her grandchildren after her only
daughter died in childbirth. She was a multifaceted
woman.

Grandma Bertha raised my great-grandmother,
Thelma. According to my great-grandmother, Grandma
Bertha could do just about anything. Since I grew up
hearing stories about the strength and versatility of
Grandma Bertha, I believe in the importance of being
multifaceted. Of course, it is important not to merely jump
from one project to the next without completion. You do
not want to be a jack of all trades but a master of none.
You have talents and gifts to share with the world in a
way no one else can share them. While it is important for

you to hone your gifts so you can fulfill your purpose and destiny, you should not be limited to only your obvious talents and gifts. You may have hidden talents which you have yet to tap into. As you go through life, you may develop an interest or become curious about something you never thought you would have liked. You might be presented with an opportunity you never expected to pursue. It is important to remain open to new ideas and always be willing to learn a new skill or technique.

One of the character traits I love about my great-grandmother is her ability to adapt to any situation. At ninety-five-years-old, she keeps up with pop culture and fashion trends. Although she has been a Christian for most of her life, she still studies the Bible, understanding there is always more to learn. While she is usually the oldest person in any given group, she can quickly acclimate to any environment. She finds enjoyment with her *Seniors on the Move* group, as well as, attending a high school football game. One of the great benefits to being multifaceted is having a richer life.

Although most colleges look for students who have a strong academic standing, they also want students to be involved in school activities, show good character, and demonstrate community service. Students who are well rounded in high school are likely to be the same in college and in life. Colleges and universities want students who are going to exceed expectations and enrich their institutions by being innovative. My academics were always my first priority, but I was active in extracurricular and community activities throughout high school and college.

In high school, I was a cheerleader, a member of Student Government, National Honor Society, Spanish Club, and Future Business Leaders of America.

Additionally, I was very active in my church, singing in the choir and participating in different community activities. In college, I lived in a scholarship house and held leadership positions in different organizations on campus. I also volunteered with Big Brothers & Big Sisters, Boys and Girls Club, and Girl Scouts. As an adult, I continue to be active and volunteer in the community.

If you are willing to constantly try new activities, you will undoubtedly meet a diverse group of people. Living in a scholarship house in college was one of the most memorable and beneficial experiences of my young adult life. My first roommate was from Ecuador. She had never been around black people and I had never heard of Ecuador. As freshmen, we learned a lot about one another and our different cultures. In total, there were seventeen young ladies living in our house and we all came from different backgrounds and had different experiences.

During my first year, there were only two phones in the house, and neither of the phones had call waiting. This was before everyone owned a cell phone. We had to wait our turn to talk when the phone was occupied and take messages for our roommates when they weren't home. We shared chores and responsibilities. Of course, we did not always agree with one another. However, we learned how to resolve conflict peacefully. It was far from being *The Bad Girls Club* ☺

The time I spent in McKaig Scholarship House was invaluable to my personal development and growth. I learned a great deal from the women with whom I lived and from the experiences we shared. As a result, I have been able to apply many of the cooperative living skills I acquired to my personal and professional life. When you open yourself up to new activities, you also open yourself to new opportunities.

When I went to college, I never thought I wanted to work in education. However, after working as an adjunct professor at Valencia Community College, I decided to make a transition into secondary education full-time. Being a licensed attorney has afforded me the opportunity to work in various capacities, including teaching at the postsecondary level and in a high school law magnet program. As a law magnet program leader, I have met with countless congressional leaders, judges, and celebrities as part of my job. It is possible I may not have experienced the same opportunities if I was solely practicing law.

One of my primary responsibilities as a law magnet program leader is to recruit new students into the program each year. I have to market the program by attending recruitment fairs, planning various activities, and showcasing what we have to offer through social media. Additionally, I spend quite a bit of time networking with local colleges, universities, organizations, and agencies to partner with the program. Consequently, I have enhanced my skills in marketing and networking, which has helped me in my personal business endeavors. If I had listened to others, however, I may not have branched out to do something beyond law. Thankfully, the lessons I learned about Grandma Bertha are a constant reminder I do not have to limit myself to one category in life.

When I was growing up, my childhood best friend's father was a great inspiration to me. He was well respected in our town and quite successful. I was always impressed by his ability to be multifaceted. While they owned an established family business, he also served as the mayor and city commissioner at different times. Additionally, he worked as a referee for local sports and owned rental property. Observing him, I learned the importance of having more than one fire burning at all times.

When you look at the wealthiest and most successful celebrities, they often are multifaceted. Jessica Simpson started out singing and displaying her life on reality television. However, she found even greater success when she branched out into other ventures. She began doing movies and launched a beauty products line, including lip glosses and fragrances. Perhaps, however, her most successful enterprise yet is her line of handbags and shoes.

Similarly, Sean Combs a.k.a. Puff Daddy a.k.a. P. Diddy began his career as an intern and talent director at Uptown Records. He went on to establish Bad Boy Entertainment and produce some of the most talented artists in the hip hop industry, including Notorious B.I.G., Mary J. Blige, and Lil' Kim. In addition to making music, Combs did some acting in films and plays, most notably *Monster's Ball* and *A Raisin in the Sun*. Combs also started a successful clothing line, as well as, a fragrance line for men. Additionally, he opened two restaurants, helped develop Cîroc vodka, and has equity in a television network. One common denominator for people who achieve wealth is diversity. Neither Simpson nor Combs limited themselves to only one avenue or path. They did not simply stay in one lane, but rather found a variety of routes for success.

The purpose for some of your choices might simply be to learn a new skill or add to your repertoire of knowledge. Other decisions may be designed to help you advance in your professional career or for personal growth.   Whether you are involved in a community service organization or you are advocating for a specific cause, choose each experience purposely to add value to your life and help you become a well-rounded individual.

BE MULTIFACETED REFLECTION

❖ Identify someone you know personally who is multifaceted. Explain what makes the person a well-rounded individual.

❖ Identify three new interests you would like to pursue (may include a business or career goal, hobby, or learning a new skill).

❖ Consider how you can diversify your life. Make a short term plan, including what steps you will take to become more well-rounded.

BE NOTEWORTHY

"If you are afraid of being forgotten, then do something memorable."
~Author Unknown

When I graduated from Bartow Senior High School, it was tradition for seniors to leave a last will and testament. The senior wills were submitted, typed up, and posted in a booklet for all seniors to read. Although it might sound morbid, it was a big deal and most seniors looked forward to it. For many, it was the opportunity to pass the torch to the underclassmen. For example, the homecoming queen may have left her crown and sash to a younger sibling to encourage her to run for the position. People often left the titles they had acquired, such as prom queen or student government president. Others left their grades or advice about taking high school seriously. The senior wills were a creative way for students to commemorate what they achieved during the four years they attended Bartow Senior High School. It was a way to be remembered.

Much like your time in high school is limited, so is your time on earth. Therefore, what you do with your time is important. You have the opportunity to leave a mark on this world based on what you do with your time, talent, and money. Recently, my friend's husband participated in a walk to bring awareness to diabetes. Because he has lived with diabetes for over seventeen years, he wanted to bring awareness to how it can be managed through proper exercise and diet. As part of his participation, he raised $10,000 for the American Diabetes Association (ADA). In order to raise the funds, he reached out to family, friends, colleagues, businesses, and organizations to support him. The ADA was so impressed with his contribution they asked him to speak at the event. Additionally, the local news station interviewed him about his involvement in the walk and bringing awareness to the cause. What he did was noteworthy! He could have been content to raise $500 or even $1000. However, he went above and beyond to make a statement. Many people suffering from diabetes will receive much needed assistance because of his efforts.

Years ago, my church used "The Greatest Gift" as the theme for our Christmas season. My pastor challenged the congregation to show unexpected and unsolicited kindness, especially to people we did not know. Some people went to local breakfast diners and left a $100 tip for their waitress. Others paid for a meal or groceries for the person in line behind them. One person even surprised a single mother with a car.

The church had a list of 200 families in need of assistance during the holidays. My pastor asked the congregation to donate 200 bicycles to ensure each family received a bicycle for Christmas. The members' generosity far exceeded what they were asked to do that holiday season. Every child in every family on the list received a bicycle and there were still hundreds of bicycles left over. When the parents arrived at the church to pick up their gifts, they were greeted by friendly church volunteers who assisted them with the registration process. Next, they were led into a toy-filled auditorium, impeccably decorated as a Christmas Wonderland. The parents were given the opportunity to select one bicycle and two smaller gifts for each child in the family.

After selecting the toys, they went to a separate room to have the toys gift wrapped by more volunteers.

While the toys were being wrapped, parents were treated to breakfast courtesy of the church. When breakfast was over, the parents picked up their gifts and a group of volunteers assisted them by helping to load the gifts into the parents' vehicle.

It took hundreds of people to effectively coordinate the event and ensure it ran successfully. The vast majority of those participating in the event were volunteers. Each volunteer could have been out shopping or spending time with her own family. However, we chose to contribute our time to make another family happy during the Christmas season. As volunteers, we were trained on how to greet the parents and make them feel welcome during the process. Our goal was to make the parents feel special and honored. Having the opportunity to participate in such an amazing event is something I will never forget. I had never witnessed the outpouring of generosity and love I witnessed during the "Greatest Gift" holiday season. Given the impact it had on me, I'm sure it was an experience those parents will never forget.

What will be your legacy? When you leave this earth, how will you be remembered? Michael Jackson will forever be known as the King of Pop. Although he faced criticism and scrutiny in his private life, his musical talent and ability was unparalleled. Long after he passed the peak of his popularity, he was still able to impact fans born decades after his music was number one on the charts. In 2015, Misty Copeland made history when she became the first African-American female principal ballet dancer for the American Ballet Theater. In over seventy-five years, they had not had an African-American female to lead the ballet company until Copeland broke the barrier. In the 2016 Rio World Olympics, Simone Biles became the most decorated American gymnast, holding a total of nineteen Olympic and World Championship medals.

Without a doubt, any person who accomplishes something great must have a strong work ethic and passion. In order to become the greatest in a particular area, you must be willing to set yourself apart from everyone else. While there is an advantage to possessing raw talent, true success is the result of how your talent is cultivated and presented to the world. Champions become champions by stretching themselves beyond the standard.

Some people never think about leaving a legacy or fulfilling their purpose in life. Perhaps you had a difficult childhood and still carry the emotional scars of what you experienced. Maybe you think you have made too many mistakes to leave any positive lasting impression on the world. You may even ask, "Who am I to do something remarkable?" My question to you would be, "Who are you not to?"

Even if no one has ever done it, you can be the first. Certainly, being the first person to do anything is a great responsibility to carry and can be downright intimidating. My great-grandmother never dreamed she would live to see the United States elect an African-American as president. However, at eighty-seven-years-old, she voted for Barack Obama and watched him become the nation's first African-American president. Four years later, she voted for him again and watched him be re-elected for a second term.

As the first African-American U.S. president, Barack Obama experienced unimaginable challenges. However, because of his willingness to take on such an incredible responsibility, my son's perspective on what he can achieve in life will be knowing a man who looked just like him was the president of the United States for eight years.

If you aspire to leave a legacy, you can expect to face adversity. Author and Bible teacher, Joyce Meyer is a prime example of someone who turned tragedy into triumph. She was sexually abused by her father for most of her childhood and teenage years. However, she has written over seventy books and has outreach ministries all over the world. Joyce shares her story of being abused and overcoming her personal challenges to help millions of people who watch her on television, attend her conferences, and read her books. She has effectively used her personal tragedy and her gift of speaking and writing to impact the lives of others.

While Joyce has solidified her legacy through her works, her brother did not do the same. In some of her teachings, she openly speaks of her brother's struggle with drug addiction for most of his adult life. According to Joyce, she and her husband tried many times to help him turn his life around. Unfortunately, her brother died of a drug overdose in an abandoned building. While they grew up in the same home, he chose to deal with his adversity differently and, unlike Joyce, left the world with little to show for what he did with his life.

Two people can live in the same home, receive the same upbringing, and live completely different lives. Many of my immediate family members and I were raised by my great-grandparents. Although we were all taught the same values, most of them chose the well-traveled path of self-indulgence and self-destruction. Thankfully, I have decided to use my pain to fulfill my purpose. When given the opportunity, I try to remind people of the talent, potential, and opportunities they have yet to uncover.

Today, I challenge you to look deep inside and discover why you were created and the gift you were meant to give the world. If you are still breathing, it means you still have time to be the brilliant, extraordinary, outstanding person you were created to be. The world is waiting for you to do something unforgettable in a positive way!

BE NOTEWORTHY REFLECTION

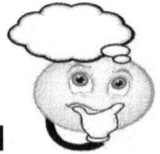

❖ If you died today, how would the people closest to you remember you? Consider three adjectives they might use to describe you.

❖ What is the most important accomplishment, achievement, or accolade you have received? Why is it the most important to you?

❖ What is a special skill or talent you possess? How have you used the special skill or talent to help others?

BE OPTIMISTIC

Don't give up and don't give in,
Although it seems you never win
You will always pass the test
As long as you keep
Your head to the sky,
Be optimistic!
~Sounds of Blackness, *Optimistic*, 1991

It was Monday morning, and Jake was having one of those days. The alarm did not go off, so he slept later than usual. His dog, PJ, had an upset stomach and left him a mess to clean. In his hurry to get out of the house, he forgot his morning coffee. On the way to work, there was an accident and he was stuck in traffic. By the time Jake finally made it to work a half hour late, he realized he had missed an important meeting. When he sat down to check his email, his computer shut down unexpectedly and locked him out of the system for an hour. At the end of the day, Jake was completely exhausted and just wanted to get home. However, when he tried to start his car, he discovered the battery was dead.

If you have a day when it seems like nothing is working in your favor, it can be easy to feel negative and discouraged. It requires much less effort to be optimistic when things are going your way. If you have money in your bank account, it is not difficult to feel hopeful about your financial future. It does not take a lot of effort to feel encouraged about your health when you receive a good report from the doctor. When you and your significant other are getting along, it is easy to feel confident in your relationship. The true test is remaining positive when your circumstances are challenging. Are you able to smile when what you owe is greater than what you have in your account? Will you keep your joy if the doctor delivers bad news? Can you focus on the positives when you go through a challenging season in your relationship?

About two years into my marriage, I had to answer those very same questions. My husband and I purchased our first house together. The time we spent looking for the house and saving for the purchase brought us closer together. We did not share our plans to buy a home with anyone until we left our closing and had the keys in our hands. While we were happy about purchasing the house, we faced some serious challenges in our marriage. I was dealing with several unexpected health issues, which put a strain on our relationship. During that period, it was hard for us to see eye to eye. I know there were days when I felt like complaining, being negative, or focusing on all that was wrong.

While I had moments when I vented out of frustration or felt down, I refused to allow it to become the norm. I knew it was a difficult season and would soon be over. When I was dealing with my health issues, I began to read healing scriptures daily and listen to inspirational messages. I looked for opportunities to surround myself with positive people and positive messages so I could remain positive. Eventually, my health improved and we were able to resolve the issues in our relationship. Sometimes the lessons you learn come from how you deal with the problem rather than the problem itself.

No matter how much money you have, how famous you are, how glamorous your life appears to be, you will not be immune to the challenges of life. However, you can still have joy in the middle of a storm. It really is about your attitude. If you do not like your job, or the people for whom you work treat you unfairly, you can still maintain a positive attitude. There are millions of unemployed people who would love to take your place. If you are overwhelmed by the responsibilities of being a parent, you can be appreciative you were able to have a child because there are many women who suffer from infertility issues and would gladly take on the responsibility. In each situation, you can choose to believe the challenges are temporary and better days are ahead.

During my teaching career, there was a period which was very difficult for me. I was under extreme pressure because the subject and grade level I was teaching was highly tested on the state examination. The school at which I was teaching was considered a low performing school under state standards. As a result, we were under constant scrutiny from district, regional, and state administrators. To make matters worse, my school administrator was not a very pleasant person.

The morale among faculty, staff, and students was very low. I can remember pulling into the parking lot and feeling dread and doom. There was not a lot of smiling or laughter happening in the building during that time. It was a dark period. I began sending out my resume and going on interviews. Even though I did not really want any of the jobs for which I was applying, I was tired of being in an oppressive situation.

While I was in the midst of my job search, I began listening to inspirational messages and teachings. I read the Bible and recited scripture throughout the day. I relied on my faith and eventually changed my attitude. I made a conscious decision to focus on what I liked about my job rather than focus on what I disliked. Soon, the feelings of doom and dread were replaced with peace and contentment. I knew I would not be in the same position forever. So, my new mantra became, "I can do anything temporarily." While I was waiting for the situation to change, I decided to be happy and positive, in the meantime.

The meantime in between time is usually the tough time. Being negative and complaining never makes any situation better. You can walk outside, see the sun shining, and think – *What a beautiful day!* Or, you can walk outside, see the sun shining and think – *Ugh! It's hot!* The choice is yours. If you train yourself to think positively and not focus on the negative in life, it does not mean everything will go your way. However, you will definitely have more peace while you are waiting for your circumstances to change.

I am generally a happy person. I enjoy smiling, laughing, and inspiring others. However, I have faced great challenges in my life for which I could have a negative perspective. I was not raised by either of my biological parents. My mother was addicted to drugs for many years and as a result, our communication was sporadic. She left me to live with my great-grandparents at five-years-old and I did not see her again until I was twenty. As a child, I was sexually abused by a distant cousin. Eventually, I informed my great-grandparents of the abuse and they protected me from the perpetrator. However, I carried emotional scars which affected my personal relationships.

At different points in my life, I have taken steps to heal and live a happier life. I have shared my story with others and sought professional therapy to move beyond my past. I could walk around feeling resentful because my biological parents were absent for much of my life. I could still be angry about being sexually abused and focus on the unfairness of it all. However, if I chose to remain angry, bitter, resentful, hurt, or disappointed, I would never be able to accomplish my destiny. Although I have felt all of those emotions at one point or another, I refuse to hang on to them and allow them to take up space in my life.

The destiny God has designed for my life requires me to be hopeful and not pessimistic. In Hebrews 11:1, the scripture says "Now faith is the substance of things hoped for; the evidence of things not seen." There are dreams God has given me and assignments for me to fulfill. I understand in order for those dreams to come to fruition, I must be patient and believe the dreams will come to pass. While you may wholeheartedly believe in what you are hoping for, it is not uncommon to feel discouraged during the wait, especially when it seems like nothing is happening. While you are waiting, it is important to monitor your thoughts and speech. If your goal is to get out of debt, you cannot walk around saying it will never happen or entertain negative thoughts about it being impossible. Be proactive about maintaining a positive attitude.

I create vision boards which depict images representative of the dreams God has placed in my heart. I align my thoughts with what God says and surround myself with positivity. In James 2:17, the scripture says "...faith by itself, if it is not accompanied by action, is dead." You should not be concerned if people don't understand your actions, especially when you are acting on faith. So, months after suffering a devastating miscarriage, I chose to demonstrate my optimism by purchasing two shirts for my son which read *Best Big Brother* and hanging them in my closet.

I know the desire for the family God placed in my heart will come to pass. Although I have not sold my first best seller yet, I know it is on the way. Choose to think and live positively. Believe the best is yet to come – because it is!

BE OPTIMISTIC REFLECTION

❖ In what area(s) of your life do you need to be more optimistic? Identify one change you can make in your daily life to help you maintain a more positive outlook.

❖ Think about a situation which did not turn out the way you expected. How did you respond at the time? What would you do differently?

❖ What is something you are hoping for in your life? Identify one step you can make to demonstrate your optimism and commit to it.

BE PRESENT

"If you are depressed, you are living in the past. If you are anxious, you are living in the future. If you are at peace, you are living in the present."
~Lao Tzu, Chinese Philosopher

When I was in my twenties, I spent much of my time looking forward to the next best thing. In between it all, I was trying to find myself. Whenever I faced disappointment, it felt like the end of the world. I distinctly remember saying – *I wish it was six months already!* If it was February, I was literally wishing for August because I wanted to move beyond the moment. It took me years to learn how to appreciate the value of the journey and the importance of being present in the moment.

Today is a day you will never get back. How will you use the time? Will you spend it mulling over past mistakes and regrets? Will you focus on your plans for next week or next month? Time is by far the most valuable resource you have because it is irreplaceable. Once it is spent, time is gone forever. For that reason, you should make the most of every moment you have. Too often people waste time by complaining about the tasks they have to complete. In most cases, they are going to end up doing them, anyway. Instead of complaining about what you have to do, you should enjoy the moment.

When I was pregnant with my son, I was working full-time. By the end of the day, I could not wait to leave work and take a nap. Each day when I arrived home, our dog, Coco, was eagerly awaiting me to take him for his evening walk. While I love little Coco to pieces, in the moment, I viewed taking him out to walk as a chore. After working all day, I didn't want to go for a walk. I wanted to take a nap! One day, while we were out, I began to look around at the scenery. There were palm trees, a lake, and birds chirping. The neighborhood was a nice area, quiet and serene. From that day forward, I decided to change my outlook. Instead of viewing the walk as something I had to do, I decided to look at walking my dog as an opportunity I was fortunate to experience. Coco was a great addition to our lives, and I was taking him for granted. I began to use my walks with Coco as a way to de-stress from the day. I learned to slow down and appreciate the trees, the birds, and just watching Coco sniff around. Once I decided to be present in the moment, I was much calmer and much happier.

There is no doubt life can be stressful and difficult at times. Most people live very busy lives, working and caring for their families. It is easy to think, "I don't have time to slow down. I have too much to do!" But, if you are always busy running from one task to the next and finishing one chore after another, it is likely you are not enjoying any of it. I have been guilty of starting one big project after another. After a while, I begin to feel burned out and overwhelmed. I have learned whenever life feels heavy it is because there is too much on my plate. When I have too much going on, I take a step back and focus on what is directly in front of me rather than what is coming up next.

A few years ago, my husband had a painful surgery which required him to be out of work for six weeks. Not long after the surgery, my husband's seventeen-year-old nephew had a stroke. Within a week of our nephew having a stroke, my uncle suffered three strokes in one week. At the same time our family members were battling serious health issues, my job became extremely demanding. With all that was going on, I was physically and emotionally drained. One day after work, my husband and I decided to take my son to the park to ride his bicycle. While we were there, we talked, laughed, and watched him ride, having the time of his life. In the moment, all of our cares were forgotten. We were not thinking about the challenges of my husband's surgery, our family members, or the issues at work. We were living in the moment.

When was the last time you were fully present in the moment? When did you last stop to watch the sun set? How long has it been since you watched the sun rise? Do you ever stand out at night and look up at the stars? There is beauty and wonder all around you. If you are too busy to notice it, you will miss out.

There will always be more work to finish at the office. In most instances, there is not enough time to complete everything on the to-do list. But, there are times when you need to press the pause button. At my job, I am not the social butterfly because I am very task-oriented. I have my to-do list and I am trying to get it done. In the past, I have had a very narrow focus and approached my job with tunnel vision. I have learned, however, the value of taking time to be present in the moment.

While working on a task I feel is very important, I might be stopped by a co-worker. Rather than treat the interruption as a disturbance or disruption, I look at it as a necessary break. In most instances, I probably needed the break but may not have taken it if my co-worker had not stopped me. If a colleague or neighbor stops by to chat while you are in the middle of something, consider whether you can spare the time before dismissing what may be an opportunity to be a blessing to someone else. The person may need a listening ear or to hear a positive word of encouragement. If you are too busy to stop, you may miss the opportunity to help someone in need. If you were on the other end, you would appreciate someone making time to be attentive to you.

In our culture, there are many things competing for our attention. Technology has made it so easy to digitally connect with people, many find it difficult to personally connect. When we go to dinner, it is not uncommon to see people more focused on their electronics than the person sitting in front of them. Being present in the moment requires you to focus on what is in front of you more than anything else, including the past.

Too often, people waste time holding on to hurts and disappointments from their past. When you refuse to let go of the fact you were wronged, you are binding yourself to the person who wronged you and the situation. For some of life's challenges, you have no control over the outcome. What you can control is how you choose to deal with it. If you choose to focus on the past, you will miss the present and limit your future.

I heard a story about a woman whose husband left her for a younger woman after many years of marriage. Devastated and hurt by his betrayal, she did not think she would find love again. Years later, she met a very nice man and they began dating. Although he was kind to her and cared for her deeply, he noticed she was still holding on to her past. She often talked about her first marriage and how she'd been betrayed. The new man in her life confided in a friend his concerns about her inability to let go of her past. Unfortunately, he eventually decided to end the relationship. In her case, she missed out on a great opportunity because her focus was on what was behind her rather than what was in front of her.

It is profound to understand the power of living in the moment. There are circumstances which happen in our lives for which we are not given a choice. You may experience a trauma, tragedy, or disappointment which cannot easily be forgiven or forgotten. People often say time heals all wounds; however, it is what you do during the time which determines whether you heal or not. If you were hurt or mistreated during your childhood, whatever happened to you is not your fault. However, you will only have yourself to blame if you continue to focus on what never was and allow it to determine what will be.

As an adult, you have likely experienced loss and heartache. If you stay focused on the past, you will be destined to repeat it. Many times, the person who caused you pain has either died, moved on, or has no idea you are still harboring resentment. While you are stuck in the past, she is living and enjoying her life. Yesterday is gone and there is no way to relive it. Tomorrow has not happened and you cannot predict it. It is more valuable to put your energy into what is happening right now.

Living in the moment and enjoying your life is a choice. Choose to appreciate this day and be present for every second. There is a reason the windshield on a car is so much larger than the rearview mirror. What you have in front of you is much greater than what you left behind!

BE PRESENT REFLECTION

❖ What two changes can you make to live a less busy lifestyle? For the next thirty days, commit to make the changes and keep a journal of how the changes improve your life.

❖ Think about someone who has hurt or disappointed you. Write the person a letter, forgiving him and releasing you from the past. You can choose to give the person the letter, keep it to yourself, or destroy it after you have written it. The point is to put the past away.

❖ What could you do in thirty minutes? Designate a time of day for which you will put aside all electronic devices and give yourself a minimum of thirty minutes to be present in the moment. Try to occupy the time with activities which require you to focus on the present (i.e. exercise, meditation, journaling).

BE QUIET

"Wise men, when in doubt whether to speak or to keep quiet, give themselves the benefit of the doubt, and remain silent."
~Napoleon Hill, American Writer

Kelsey, a successful business executive at a major advertising agency was accustomed to having a busy schedule. Most of her mornings were spent in meetings and working on various projects to present to potential clients. When she was not in a meeting or giving a presentation, she was working on negotiating a deal or consulting with her team to prepare for the next project.

Kelsey's day usually began at 5:00 a.m. with her making a quick breakfast, helping her daughter get dressed for school, getting dressed for work, and rushing out the door by 6:45 a.m. On most days, she tried to drop her daughter off to the before-care program by 7:15 a.m. and make it to her office by 8:00 a.m. In the afternoon, she tried to leave the office by 5:30 p.m. and pick her daughter up from dance class by 6:00 p.m. Once she made it home, Kelsey and her husband routinely recapped their day while Kelsey started dinner.

After dinner, they took turns reviewing their daughter's homework with her. When Kelsey was not assisting with homework, she was busy checking her work emails and responding to the most pressing issues. Before bed, Kelsey liked to read her daughter a book and ensure her daughter's clothes for the next school day were ready. By the time she got into bed, Kelsey was exhausted and usually fell asleep as soon as her head hit the pillow.

Scheduling a time for peace and quiet is essential to your well-being. Where was the down time? Where were the quiet moments in Kelsey's busy day? You might suggest on the drive to and from work. While you may be able to get quiet on the way to work in traffic and on the way home during rush hour, you still have to be alert because you are driving. Sometimes quiet is as much about your state of mind as what is going on around you.

Whether you are a college student, single entrepreneur, or stay at home mom, most people live busy lives. High school and college students have classes, extracurricular activities, and in many cases, a part-time job. Many college students work full-time while going to school part-time. Working people often have more responsibilities than they can manage during the workday. If you are a parent, taking care of a child is a job itself.

Throughout the day, most people are on their cell phones emailing, texting, and posting on social media. Multi-tasking is an expected skill for today's job market. The fact our country needed to create laws to ban texting while driving is a clear indication of how hectic our lives have become.

When you have a busy schedule, there is little time for quiet or self-reflection because you are constantly running from one thing to the next. However, in order to sustain a healthy lifestyle you must allow time to be refreshed and renewed. When I was in high school and college, my schedule was packed with classes, extracurricular activities, and community involvement. After I graduated from college, I was focused on law school. When I finished law school, I was busy studying for the bar exam. Once I passed the bar exam, my goal was to find an apartment and start my career. It did not take long for me to realize life would not stop or slow down unless I made a conscious decision to slow down. As an author and speaker, I constantly have ideas floating around in my mind. It is not uncommon for me to get up in the middle of the night to right down an idea. It can be difficult to turn off the creative process. As a result, I had to discover ways to relax, refresh, and renew.

Some days, the noise around me is deafening. After a long day at work, my husband is asking a million questions, Tristan is running through the house, and Coco is barking at the wind. Deadlines and my to-do list may be swirling around in my head. On those days, I steal away to my bathroom and take a long, hot, bubble bath. With candles lit around me, I allow myself to escape in the water. Although the bath may only last for twenty minutes, it is an opportunity to experience a much needed respite from reality.

You have to establish methods to ensure you have a sense of peace in life. Exercise can also be a great way to clear your mind and relieve stress. Running, especially, is one way I reduce pressure and anxiety in my life. After a good workout, whatever was bothering me prior to the workout has usually been resolved. Working out gives me the opportunity to get quiet and surrender my thoughts.

The beach is also a great option when you need tranquility. The sound of the ocean instantly puts my mind at ease. Whether I am running along the beach or enjoying a beach day, listening to the waves helps me to transition to a peaceful mood. I feel centered and more at peace because while I am watching the waves, I'm usually not thinking about much else other than the wonder of God's creation. I usually silence my phone so I can spend the time relaxing and reflecting. Sometimes, I take reading material or sit and observe the scenery. Other times, I use my beach day to journal. Whenever I go to the beach, it is an opportunity to be reenergized through the tranquility and serenity of my surroundings. It is important for me to take the time to renew myself because I spend a great amount of time working on various projects for my job, my business, and my family. Without the quiet, I would not be as effective as I need to be in the various facets of my life.

While being quiet is often about your environment and state of mind, there are also times when it is a necessary action. My first experience serving on a jury was quite interesting. I was selected, along with six other people, to serve on a jury trial which lasted four days. On the first day, we were given instructions to listen to the evidence and not to discuss the case until the trial was over. There were several times during the trial when we were asked to go to the jury room while the attorneys presented issues to the judge. As we were dismissed each time, the judge reminded us not to discuss the case until the end of the trial. However, as soon as the bailiff closed the door, one of the jurors immediately began talking about the case. He started by stating his opinion. Then, he began to ask another juror questions. By the end of the third day, he was even talking during the actual trial. While the attorneys were questioning witnesses, he was making comments in the jury box. No matter what was happening around him, he could not be quiet.

If you are prone to complaining, it is absolutely better to stay quiet. Certainly, if you are surrounded by people who gossip, nitpick, or criticize, you might consider finding a different group. At the very least, you can choose to zip it. Joining in the conversation may lead to unwanted consequences. The person complaining or gossiping may take what you say in the conversation and spread it around to others. Or, even worse, your words could be twisted around and presented with a completely different meaning than you originally intended. However, if you choose to remain quiet, you may keep yourself from becoming entangled in chaos and trouble. There are times when you must speak your mind or take a stand. I am definitely not suggesting you remain silent when you see someone being mistreated or if your beliefs are being challenged. However, you must determine when it is necessary to speak up or stay quiet.

There will definitely be instances in your life when silence is the better option. You may set a goal which seems impossible to most, but you know in your heart you are supposed to accomplish it. Sharing your dream with everyone is not necessary because everyone will not be supportive or understand you. If you share your aspirations with the wrong people, they may try to discourage you from moving forward. For example, if you are currently working a job paying minimum wage and have a goal to buy a home, it might look impossible to an outsider. You may believe God placed the dream in your heart and have the faith it will come to fruition. However, if you begin to share the dream prematurely with people who are not supportive, they may try to talk you out of it because they are doubtful.

It should not be surprising for someone who does not share your same vision, belief, or level of faith to be unsupportive. You should never take "No" from someone who is not in a position to give you a "Yes." Therefore, you should be selective with whom you share the goals and aspirations of your heart.

When people fast, they do it as a sacrifice and a way to hear from God. Sometimes, the only way to hear from God is to get quiet and remove yourself from the distractions of your daily life. You were not given two ears and one mouth by mistake. There is a need for silence in your life. Without silence, there can be no true self-reflection. Whether it is a retreat to the mountains, silencing your cell phone, serene walks on the beach, or a long, hot, bubble-bath, make peace and quiet in your life a priority. Your heart and mind will thank you!

BE QUIET REFLECTION

❖ Consider your current method for refreshing and reenergizing. What are some ways you can achieve more peace and quiet in your life?

❖ During the next thirty days, try to incorporate the methods you listed above into your daily lifestyle. Monitor whether you notice positive changes.

❖ Think about a time when you spoke but should have been quiet. What was the effect of you speaking? How could you have handled the situation differently?

BE RESILIENT

"Keep your head up. God gives his hardest battles to
his toughest soldiers."
~Author Unknown

*I remember feeling excited that day. I had not felt
much excitement since taking the initial test which turned
out to be positive. For the past twelve weeks, I had felt
nauseous and exhausted pretty much every day. My
nerves were on edge, and I was definitely hormonal. But,
that day, I was excited. I arrived at the doctor's office
ready to hear my baby's heartbeat and eager to discuss
the next phase. As I prepared to go inside, I reached for
my blazer resting in the passenger seat of my truck. But,
I put it back thinking, "I'm 14 weeks now and proud. I'm
going to show off my baby bump!"*

*In the waiting room, I passed the time by catching
up with my friend over the phone. It had been at least a
week since we'd spoken and I wanted to know what was
going on with her. We chatted for about half an hour and
then the nurse, called me in. Following the usual routine,
she took my weight, told me to leave a urine sample, and
directed me to the exam room. When my doctor finally
arrived, she was as happy to see me as I was to see her.
The last visit had been emotional because I was feeling
so sick and miserable. I had actually started crying and
needed a pep talk during our last visit.*

"My Asiah is back!" my doctor exclaimed.

"I know! I feel so much better," I said with a smile.

*I asked her a few questions about having my tubes
tied and she shared her experience. What an amazing
doctor! She was always transparent about her struggles*

and fears as a woman, which has a very calming effect for a nervous patient. Then, it was on to my exam.   Like always, I was a little nervous, or maybe anxious is a better word, right before hearing the heartbeat. When it seemed to take longer than normal, I just told myself not to get concerned. My doctor wasn't frantic, but she was focused. Determined. And, then, I could see concern on her face. But, still, I told myself not to get worried. "He's in there. Just hiding," I thought. She took me into another examination room and tried again.

I could see the screen and her face said it was bad, so I asked, "Is it bad?"

She couldn't look at me. She just said, "I'm sorry."

In between tears and gut wrenching cries, I asked, "Could you be wrong? Could you be wrong?"

It was the most unexpected, devastating news I have ever received.

There are moments in life which drop us to our knees. Losing my child at fourteen weeks was one of those moments. There is no real explanation for why it happened. *Sometimes, there is an insufficient number of chromosomes at the time of conception. Sometimes, there is something which causes the baby not to develop. You didn't do anything wrong. There was nothing you could do. These things happen.* These were the explanations I received.

As a Christ follower, I believe in the Word of God. But this life event shook my faith at its core. Like any believer, after suffering a tragedy, I looked to God for answers, but I did not receive any immediately. Spiritually, I felt alone. Where was God? Why wasn't he answering my call? Why couldn't I feel him near? There were definitely more questions than answers, and I had received a response to none. The one question I did not ask was – *Why me?* I knew too many women who had suffered the same terrible loss, albeit different circumstances. They were good women with good hearts, hopes, and dreams. We were now part of a sisterhood none of us asked to join. My questions were more related to the lesson and the journey. Why this lesson? Why this way? Why this journey? How was this going to work together for my good? Why answer my prayer and then take it away? Did God answer my prayer? It was a season of confusion.

People often tell others to be strong during a tragedy. What does such strength look like? I cried every day for weeks. Did my tears mean I was weak? I was no longer pregnant, but the pain of the loss was a constant presence. The days immediately after are a blur of being wide awake in a daze. My eyes were open, but it took a while to fully grasp what had happened. I knew I had to do the basics, like brush my teeth and shower, which I did, begrudgingly. Perhaps, one of the most difficult aspects was letting go of the dream. Making the mental shift from being pregnant to not being pregnant was incredibly challenging. While pregnant, I had made mental preparations of things I needed to do in the coming months. Now what? I had mentally adjusted to what I could not do while pregnant and had become accustomed to the routine. Without notice, everything had changed.

Watching my body attempt to go back to its pre-pregnancy state was frustrating. I woke up several times thinking it was all a bad dream. Instinctively, I touched my stomach and realized it was very much real. I envied people around me being able to laugh and find humor in everyday life. I longed for the joy and peace I felt prior to

March 2, 2016. I knew it would eventually return, but in the moment it felt very far away.

When you suffer a loss, experience a tragedy, or live through a traumatic experience, it leaves a permanent mark, like a tattoo. Your life is forever changed. Only you can determine whether it is for the better or worse. Sorrow is not permanent and grief is not forever. They each serve a purpose in the process. Sometimes, I felt angry and wanted to scream and punch the walls. Other times, I felt extremely sad and cried a river of silent tears. Through it all, I tried to remember I was still here. I was still living because God has a purpose for my life which is yet to be fulfilled. I had to remind myself of all for which I had to be thankful rather than constantly focusing on what I did not have.

Resilience does not come from the ability to hold in your emotions or true feelings. Let it out! You'll feel better once you do. True resilience comes from having the courage to acknowledge every emotion you feel and trust there will be better days ahead. I am deeply moved when I hear someone has taken his life because notwithstanding mental illness, he had to feel such a level of despair and such a lack of hope. When you are going through it, you must look for hope in what is around you. There are others who have faced similar and worse situations. When you can reflect on the pain someone else has experienced and see them still standing, it should provide a sense of hope and encouragement.

Think back over your life. Surely, there have been other challenges you faced and endured. Despite how difficult it was at the time, you made it through the difficulty and moved into a different season of life. If you did it once, you can do it again. Remember, no matter how bad your situation may seem, there is always someone else who would love to trade their problems for yours.

There are some experiences in life you will never forget. However, the very nature of life requires you to move forward. There is a tendency to want it to be over already; however, in my experience, what you choose to do in the time will determine when the grieving process will end. I have found strength in allowing myself time to feel sad, to grieve, to be angry, and to wonder. I allowed myself to feel the pain and cried out loud when it felt unbearable.

There were times when I needed to be alone and found a quiet place to be with myself. I journaled my thoughts because it helped me process what I was feeling. Eventually, I shared my feelings with those closest to me so they could understand the type of support I needed. The people around you want to make it better, but they do not always know what to say or do. In many circumstances, there are no words or actions which will take away your pain or make it better. It can be helpful to let those who love you off the hook and express what type of support you need.

I also met with my therapist, which I had done during other challenging points in my life. Sometimes having an objective third party ask the right questions will help you reach a conclusion or realization you might not have reached on your own. Finally, I found strength in focusing on my blessings. God has continuously blessed me. Even in my darkest hour, I could not ignore all the blessings I have received.

By focusing on what I have, I remained in the present. I did not want to lose precious time focusing all of my energy on what could have been, but was not. At some point in the grieving process, I had to make a conscious mind shift to focus my attention on my purpose in life – why I am still here, rather than why such an unfortunate event happened in my life. It was difficult to do. There were times when I had to make a list of my blessings, read stories of those less fortunate, and reflect on my own words of encouragement. I have found resilience by living out the faith I have shared with others. My resilience has come from walking out the words I have used to empower others to keep going. Giving up was never an option for me and neither should it be for you.

You may never understand why *it* happened. But, as long as you are breathing, you can get through it. You are stronger than you think. Whatever the circumstance, you are going to be even stronger for having overcome it. Look forward to brighter days ahead. They are coming!

BE RESILIENT REFLECTION

❖ What is a great challenge, obstacle, or difficulty you have faced in life? What steps did you take to overcome it?

❖ What did you learn from the experience? How did you grow as a result of it?

❖ Think of something you strongly desire to have. If you never receive it, how will you deal with the disappointment?

BE SUPPORTIVE

"You can do anything as long as you have the passion, the drive, the focus, and the support."
~Sabrina Bryan, American Actress and Singer

When I was pregnant with my son, Tristan, we waited until our three month checkup to announce the pregnancy. Living in South Florida, my husband and I were alone and away from our family. We went home for the weekend and asked the family to meet for dinner. Just before we started eating, I asked everyone to pose for a photo. As soon as it was time to snap the photo, I announced we were expecting a baby. The family was overjoyed!

Once Tristan was born, my great aunt and great-grandmother moved in with us temporarily to help us adjust to life with a newborn. Originally, they were only supposed to be with us for a few months, but they ended up staying for a year and a half. During the time they lived with us, they assisted by cooking, cleaning, and helping to care for our son. Without their support, we would have had to place Tristan in daycare much earlier, which would also have cost us almost $1000/month.

English Poet, John Donne, said "No man is an island, entire of itself." None of us can do life alone without the assistance of someone else. No matter how independent or self-sufficient you are, you will need someone for something as you journey through life. While it is good to have the support of others, it is also good to be supportive of someone else. When you see someone smiling, you do not know the story behind the smile. Every individual has experienced a hardship or disappointment. Every person has his own story.

Instead of writing someone off as having had an easy life or making the assumption she could never understand your situation, you should look at her life and be supportive.

During a staff meeting, our administration showed a video of people working in various roles at a high school. In the video, the principal was worried about his wife who had been diagnosed with cancer and was undergoing chemotherapy. Although he was concerned about his wife, no one around him knew what he was going through personally. Likewise, his secretary was secretly stressed out because her son had been arrested and was facing serious criminal charges.

Down the hall, one of the counselors was late for the third time in a week because her car broke down and needed major repairs. While she was doing her best to help students, her mind was focused on how her husband would get to work because the pair shared one car. On the other side of campus, unbeknownst to his colleagues, a teacher was starting the day with a broken heart because his wife had served him with divorce papers the night before. Another teacher was concerned because she had an overdrawn bank account with outstanding payments pending and no money in her savings account.

In the same school, there were several students in the office waiting to be issued late passes to class. One student was late because her mom had moved across town to escape an abusive boyfriend, but wanted to keep her daughter in the same school with her friends. Another student was late because his mom worked nights and he was responsible for getting his younger siblings to school on time. The attendance clerk signing the passes was not in the best mood. She had gone to the doctor the day before and received news she would need to have knee surgery. The recovery would require her to be out for six weeks and she did not have short-term disability insurance. Unfortunately, the registrar was dealing with the news her mother, who lived with her, had early signs of dementia.

The faculty, staff, and students at the school were all juggling their responsibilities and their personal challenges without the people around them knowing. While the examples might seem extreme, if you were to poll people working in any office, you would likely get a similar result. You should not take for granted all is well with a person because he shows up and does his job. At any given moment, we all are preparing to enter a storm, in the eye of a storm, or coming out of a storm.

Despite what you see on the outside, every person has a struggle of his own. Whenever you can be a source of strength, support, or encouragement, you should take the opportunity. You never know how your show of support can affect someone's situation. I heard a story about a cashier working in a local grocery store. One particular afternoon, her line was backed up and moving extra slowly. The customers were complaining and becoming noticeably impatient. As the customers reached the register, they made negative comments and were downright rude to the woman ringing up their groceries. However, one gentleman in the line decided he was going to do something different.

Rather than complain and become impatient, he decided to have a positive attitude and encourage the young woman. When he made it to the register, he encouraged her to take her time and praised her for doing an excellent job. To his surprise, she burst into tears. The man thought he had said something wrong, and undoubtedly, so did everyone else in line observing the situation.

Seeing his employee in tears, the manager of the store rushed over to see what had transpired between the cashier and the customer. Between her tears, the cashier explained the customer had not done anything wrong. She told how her little boy was in the hospital and all she could think about was whether he was doing okay. She had not been able to concentrate on her job because she was worried about her son's health. While other customers had been rude and unforgiving, it was the encouragement and unsolicited kindness of one man which put her at ease. For the first time since her son had been hospitalized, the cashier felt a sense of peace and hope.

There are different ways to offer support. If you notice a friend struggling with an issue, you can offer to help or direct him to the proper resources which would offer the support he needs. When there is a new hire on your job, a friendly face can open the door for questions or make the person feel welcome. You can also be a listening ear when someone is going through a difficult time or has to make an important decision.

Years ago, a colleague, whom I will call Tanya, was concerned about the actions of another colleague, whom I will call Lisa. Tanya worked hard and was often praised for her results. Lisa was also a hard worker, but usually did not achieve the same results as Tanya. There were several instances when Lisa gave backhanded compliments or made indirect references which Tanya believed were digs toward her and the success she had experienced. Unfortunately, Tanya strongly believed Lisa had a jealous spirit and felt her negativity was affecting the department. Tanya came to me on different occasions throughout the year to express her concerns and frustrations. While there were times when I offered advice to Tanya, most times I simply provided a supportive listening ear. I never shared the information Tanya communicated to me with anyone else because it was shared in confidence.

Having an inner circle with whom you can share your thoughts, ideas, dreams, fears, and frustrations is a key element of support. If you have a dream or goal, it is important to have an accountability partner. Your accountability partner is someone who will motivate you, encourage you, and challenge you as you are working toward achieving your goals. The person who supports you could be a good friend, mentor, coach, spouse, or significant other. When you lack confidence, your accountability partner should remind you of the obstacles you have overcome in the past and encourage you to keep moving forward.

Sometimes, showing support does not require you to say or do anything other than be present. Giving encouragement by cheering the loudest or simply just being present in the room are both ways to be supportive. When I have a speaking engagement, it is always encouraging to see my husband in the audience. It does not matter how many times he has heard the speech before, his presence alone gives me a boost of confidence and is a source of strength when I need it most.

Although it is important to be supportive by offering encouragement, there are times when words alone are insufficient for the situation in front of you. When a person experiences tragedy, people usually offer condolences. It is not uncommon for people to say things like, "Everything happens for a reason" or "You have to be strong." As you encourage others and show support, remember each individual is unique and every situation is different. Saying the wrong thing at the wrong time can definitely do more harm than saying nothing at all. Sometimes it is better to offer your presence as a source of support and just be silent.

When you face your own challenges, one of the best ways to overcome is by doing something for another person in need. When you offer genuine support, you shift the focus from yourself to someone else. Regardless of your social status or financial situation, no one is exempt from needing others.

In the movie, *Crash*, Sandra Bullock played Jean Cabot, the rich, self-absorbed wife of a California District Attorney. Throughout the movie, Jean showed little emotion or concern for anyone other than herself. After she was carjacked by two black men at gunpoint, she became angry and bitter toward minorities. Only after Jean was physically injured from a fall and needed help, did she realize she was all alone. The Hispanic housekeeper, to whom Jean had been disrespectful and condescending, was the one who eventually came to her aid. In a moment of brutal honesty, Jean wrapped her arms around the housekeeper and declared she was the only real friend Jean had in her life. The scene is a poignant example of how none of us can go through life and make it alone. We need each other to survive!

BE SUPPORTIVE REFLECTION

❖ Who is your accountability partner? How has your accountability partner been supportive of your endeavors?

❖ For whom have you been an accountability partner? How can you be more supportive of the people in your life?

❖ In what areas of life do you need more support? What is one thing your accountability partner can do to support you with your present goals?

BE TRANSPARENT

"Honesty and transparency make you vulnerable. Be honest and transparent anyway."
~Mother Theresa, Catholic Nun and Missionary

Christopher, a young attorney, was seeking a job with a posh law firm. Although he did well in law school, he knew finding a job with a prestigious firm could be a challenge. He was elated when he received an offer to become a junior associate attorney with one of the larger firms in the area. Christopher did not come from a wealthy family and made his way through college and law school by attaining scholarships, working part-time jobs, and taking out student loans.

Not long after starting his job with the firm, Christopher observed most of the attorneys wore expensive suits and drove luxury vehicles, which they had detailed in the firm's private garage. Wanting to fit in, he decided to splurge on an expensive wardrobe. After being with the firm for a couple of months, Christopher also decided it was time to upgrade to a top of the line luxury car. Shortly after purchasing his brand new car, Christopher moved into a high rise apartment building overlooking the bay.

By all accounts, Christopher was living his dream. Whether he was walking into a room or driving down the street, he looked like someone who was making moves. During his first year as a junior associate, Christopher was assigned to work on a big case for the firm. Richard, one of the senior partners asked him to conduct research on a legal issue and put together a presentation for the senior partner's team. Although Christopher was excited to be trusted with the task, he knew it was a very important case and was nervous about making a mistake.

One week before the presentation, Jason, one of the attorneys working on the case, called Christopher into his office. Jason had been with the firm for seven years and was on track to become a partner. He wanted to make sure Christopher wasn't overwhelmed by the assignment he'd been given. When Jason asked Christopher if he needed help or had any questions about the research, Christopher assured Jason he had covered all the bases and was simply tweaking the presentation. Jason even offered to have another associate work with Christopher during the last few days to ensure no stone was left unturned.

Although the legal issue Christopher had been asked to research was more complex than he'd initially thought, Christopher did not want to give Jason the impression he needed help. Although Christopher could have really benefited from having a partner, he declined the assistance. Instead, Christopher guaranteed Jason he had it all under control and the team would be pleased.

On the morning of the presentation, Christopher presented the research he'd found, carefully pointing out specific details which would help or harm the firm's case. Unbeknownst to Christopher, Jason had assigned Emily, another associate to conduct research, as well. When Christopher concluded his presentation, Emily spoke up about a loophole she'd discovered which could potentially change the outcome of the case.

Christopher was surprised to hear Emily had been assigned to do the same research and suddenly regretted not accepting Jason's offer of help. After the meeting, Richard and Jason met with Christopher to discuss his work on the case. While they commended his effort, they warned him of how one mistake could cost the firm millions of dollars. It was a lesson Christopher never forgot.

How could Christopher have handled his situation differently? Although he had mastered the appearance of being a big shot, he still had quite a bit to learn. His failure to be honest about needing help could have cost the firm millions and may have cost him his reputation. We have all been in a position where we want to impress others or present a certain image. In this case, Christopher was afraid to admit he needed help. He might have been concerned his superiors would think he wasn't qualified to handle the task. It is also possible he declined the offer of help because he wanted to receive all the credit for the work. Either way, he misrepresented the situation and it almost cost him a great deal. Ironically, if he had accepted the help, the loophole may have been accredited to the work he and Emily did together. However, Christopher would have needed to be transparent and it was not something he was willing to do.

If you look up the word transparent, you will find the following synonyms: see-through, clear, translucent, obvious, apparent, visible, and evident. There is definitely an aspect of vulnerability to being transparent. When you make a decision to be transparent, you choose not to hide a particular part of your life. It can be unnerving because you give up your privacy in a way and put yourself at risk to be judged or to lose whatever you might be trying to hold. In Christopher's case, being transparent would have made it apparent he was learning and growing like every other new attorney. However, he wanted to hold on to the image he'd created, which most people probably saw through, anyway. We all have fears, doubts, and feelings of inadequacy at some point in life. In most instances, when you try to hide or cover what is real, life has a way of exposing the truth. It really is easier to make sure what you show on the surface is consistent with what dwells on the inside.

I have often heard people in church say, "If you talk the talk, you must walk the walk." In other words, if you say you are a Christian or proclaim to live a Christian life, what you do in private should not be completely inconsistent with what you do in public. By no means, am I suggesting any Christian or any person is perfect in any way. I mess up daily! And, I'm sure you do, as well ☺ However, in your quest to grow and become a better person, you must try to learn from your mistakes to avoid continually repeating them. American author, H. Jackson Brown, Jr. said, "Our character is what we do when we think no one is looking." Do the people in your life know the true you? Are you a completely different person depending on who is in the room? You may wear many hats and reserve certain personality traits for those with whom you have a close or personal relationship. However, your core values should remain intact no matter the group or situation.

Not long ago, I walked into the grocery store with a list, determined to stick to my budget. However, when I turned the corner I spotted a delightful sight. There was a bright, red sale sign on one of my favorite foods, Dungeness crab legs. Unfortunately, crab legs were not on my list. Yet, I made an exception since the Dungeness crab legs were rarely ever on sale. The young man in the seafood department rang up the crab legs and handed me the tray. When I looked at the sticker, I noticed the price on the sticker was much lower than it should be. I had a couple of pounds of crab legs and the price was the equivalent of what a little over one pound might cost. I had a decision to make, and I had a budget to keep. I thought for a second, *Maybe this is a blessing. God knows how much I love these crab legs. And, he certainly knows my budget.* However, I was immediately convicted because I knew the price was wrong.

Of course, God can bless me anyway he chooses. But, I have never known God to bless in a way which was deceitful. If I took the crab legs, I would be stealing, and in my heart, I knew it was wrong. The young man did not seem to realize he had made the mistake. If he was reprimanded for making the mistake, I did not want it to be on my conscience. I also did not want to miss out on a true blessing because I chose to take an unwarranted discount on some crab legs.

"Have a nice day," the young man said with a smile.

"Um, I think you made a mistake," I said, handing him back the tray of crab legs.

"What do you mean?" he asked.

"You charged me a lot less for these crab legs than they really cost," I told him.

"Wow! You're right," he said, clearly unaware of his mistake.

He proceeded to call the manager over to correct the price. He thanked me for my honesty and handed me the same tray of crab legs with a much more expensive sticker price attached. Although I did not stick to my budget, I did stick to my values. I left the store feeling thankful I had chosen to be transparent and do the right thing.

There are going to be days when your character is tested. Sometimes the test may come in the form of a grocery store dilemma. Other times, it may be a situation far greater which puts all you have worked for in jeopardy. Do not allow pride, greed, envy, jealousy, or fear to keep you from making the right decisions. Being transparent requires you to be vulnerable. For most people, being vulnerable is an uncomfortable position. When you are willing to be uncomfortable, however, you can learn life's greatest lessons. If you are wearing a mask for fear of failure, make a decision today to remove the mask and live authentically. Whether you know it or not, someone is watching you. They will learn from you and your experiences, but only if they can really see you.

BE TRANSPARENT REFLECTION

❖ Think about your character and what makes you who you are. Write a paragraph in third person introducing <u>YOUR NAME HERE</u> to the world. Consider your strengths, weaknesses, goals, and fears.

❖ Consider a time when you were not as transparent as you should have been. Why did you avoid being transparent? What would you do differently?

❖ In what area(s) of your life could you be more transparent? What is stopping you from revealing more of your true self to others?

BE UNDETERRED

"No one can make you feel inferior without your consent."
~Eleanor Roosevelt, Former First Lady and Author

As a speaker, I always look for ways to challenge myself and improve my skills. I have been a member of Toastmasters International, Inc. off and on for many years. In an effort to incorporate more humor into my presentations, I participated in the District Humorous Speech Contest. While I do not particularly consider myself a funny person, I know humor is incredibly effective in speaking. When I entered the room, it was buzzing with speakers and spectators. I looked around trying to find a place to sit. Eventually, I found a seat among the other contestants. While they all appeared to be incredibly confident and poised, I was pretty nervous.

One of the contestants approached me and asked, "Are you in the contest?"

I replied, "Yes."

She responded with a disingenuous, "Good luck."

When I took the stage, I could feel my nerves for the first five seconds. However, once I began the speech and people started laughing, my nervousness went away. I knew I was doing what I was gifted for and what I had spent hours preparing to do.

When the contest was over, the same speaker stopped me and said, "Congratulations! You were great!" This time, she seemed sincere.

"Thanks," I said smiling and holding my first place trophy.

When I first entered the room, I did not feel bold. In fact, I felt intimidated by the other contestants. I had seen many of them speak before, and I knew they were good speakers. However, I also knew feeling intimidated was not going to help me win. Rather than focus on what I knew about the other contestants, I had to focus on what I knew about myself. I knew I was a good writer and speaker, as well. I also knew I was prepared and would give it my very best. If I did not have confidence in myself, I'm sure I would not have won the Humorous Speech Contest. I had to believe in myself and what I was saying if I wanted the audience to believe in me.

One mistake many people make is allowing others to intimidate them or being intimidated by others' success. You can accomplish just as much as the next person as long as you are willing to do what it takes to be successful. When a bold person steps into the room, he attracts attention because confidence is attractive. People are drawn to those who are sure of themselves. There is a fine line between confidence and arrogance. Confidence says, "I know who I am. I know what I want. I will work hard to make it happen." Arrogance says, "You should know who I am. You should know what I want. You should be willing to do whatever I want you to do to make it happen." Confidence says, "I love and value me." Arrogance says, "You should love and value me." There is nothing attractive about arrogance because arrogance is more about ego rather than believing in you.

There will always be opportunities to doubt your talent, potential, and ability. However, you have to silence the haters and trust in what you have to offer. When I was preparing for the humorous speech contest, I thought to myself, *Who is going to laugh at this? I'm not even funny.* However, I kept on writing and practicing my speech, even when I felt doubtful. There were times when I thought, *What if no one laughs? What if I get on the stage and hear crickets?* However, I remained undeterred in the midst of my fear.

You can mistakenly believe those who are successful and accomplish their dreams do so without ever feeling afraid. I have given hundreds of presentations in front of various sized crowds. No matter how many times I speak or the size of the audience, I am always nervous before I take the stage. However, I have never allowed my nervousness, anxiety, fear, or doubt to keep me from doing whatever I want to do. When you see people doing whatever they do, you should not assume they don't have any fears. Successful people refuse to allow fear to be a hindrance.

In the Bible, David was only a boy when he defeated the giant, Goliath. His own father counted him out and dismissed him as a possibility to fight Goliath. Most people would have laughed at the thought of this small boy taking down a great giant. However, David was bold. He had confidence in himself men twice his age did not have. He believed he could defeat the giant, even when others doubted him. Do you have the confidence of David? Or, are you walking around with a spirit of doubt and fear?

As I stated in an earlier chapter, I wanted to be a rapper when I was younger. During one summer, a close friend heard about a talent show in a neighboring town. She and I wrote a rap and practiced it for weeks. On the night of the talent show, her mother drove us to the community center where it was being held. When we walked into the auditorium, it was dark and loud, with music blaring. The attendees were obviously high school age, much older than me and my friend.

My friend's mother turned to us and said, "This is a much older crowd. Are you sure you want to do this?"

140

Without any hesitation, I responded, excitedly, "Yes!" I knew they were older, but I was undeterred. We had practiced for weeks, and I believed we were ready.

However, after scanning the crowd, my friend quickly decided she was not going to take the stage. No matter how much I pleaded with her, she was not willing to participate in the show. On the way home, I thought about what might have happened. It is highly likely we would have lost the talent show. Looking back, my ability to rhyme was not my strongest skill☺. We may have even been booed from the stage. However, what bothered me most was I would never know. Since we never took the stage, I did not have a chance to discover what could have happened. While it was only a community talent show and I was just a kid, I learned an important lesson. Everyone you meet will not be as courageous, bold, or confident as you. Even at eleven, I did not like the idea of being limited by my fears or being limited by someone else's.

A bold person may also be described as being brave, daring, courageous, valiant, gallant, unflinching, forward, self-assured, or confident. In order to move to the next level or accomplish the goals you have in life, you will have to be brave at some point. Your act of courage might be pitching a new idea to an investor. Or, it could be taking a job in a new city. You may have to step out of your comfort zone and volunteer to lead a new project. Maybe even speaking in front of an audience is a gutsy move for you. Whatever you do, you should never allow fear to stop you from moving forward. Your level of promotion in life is often determined by your willingness to be uncomfortable. As long as you are content in your position, you will remain exactly where you are.

Making the decision to find my father was one of my more courageous moments. As a child, I never saw a picture of him, or even knew his name. However, I decided to look for him in my late twenties. As I gathered information, I found out his name, a nickname, his occupation, and the city in which he lived. Armed with very little information, I made a list of phone numbers using the Internet and 411. I did not have a plan for what I was going to say if one of the numbers turned out to be his. I was quite aware he might reject me, ridicule me, or even deny me. It was possible none of the numbers were his, and I did not have a plan for that possibility either. I proceeded, undeterred, knowing failure and rejection were possible. In the end, I found my father and the closure I needed to resolve an important chapter in my life. However, I never would have been able to get closure if I had not been bold enough to take the risk.

Don't go through life so afraid to take chances you miss out on important opportunities. If you never take a risk, you will never gain anything. I once read Beyoncé is actually very shy and has an alter ego she calls Sasha Fierce. Once she takes the stage, she goes into Sasha Fierce mode, which enables her to be the dynamic performer you see on stage. If you need to create an alter ego to walk boldly with confidence, then get started. Make the decision today you will not allow fear, intimidation, or doubt to stand in the way of you becoming everything you were created to be. What could you do if you weren't afraid? Whatever your answer, do it anyway!

BE UNDETERRED REFLECTION

❖ Think of a situation in which you felt intimidated or fearful in the past. What was the source of intimidation or fear? What was the outcome?

❖ In what area(s) of your life do you feel bold? Explain why you feel bold in the area(s) of your life.

❖ What is one area in your life where you need to have more confidence? What steps can you take to demonstrate boldness in this area of your life?

BE VIGILANT

"Be sober, be vigilant; because your adversary the devil walks about like a roaring lion, seeking whom he may devour."
~ 1 Peter 5:8 NKJV

Nothing affects a mother more than an issue involving her child. We were only twelve days into the New Year when I received the phone call.

"Mrs. Manning, we gave Tristan an assessment and he did not do well on it at all," the teacher informed me.

"What do you mean?" I asked.

The teacher cleared her throat.

"I mean, he doesn't demonstrate mastery in phonetic awareness. He only knows four letters and sounds. He can identify six additional letters by sight, but he cannot identify the sound it makes."

"Are you sure he was taking the assessment seriously?" I asked in a concerned tone.

"I asked him to tell me what sound the letter makes and he didn't know it. At first, I thought he was playing. But, when he continued to get them wrong, I realized he really doesn't know."

"What do I need to do?" I asked. "We are working with him at home every night. This is surprising to me," I told the teacher, feeling confused.

"Asiah, we need to come up with a plan to get him where he needs to be. When I went home last night, I felt depressed. I couldn't believe he scored so poorly. I thought I was going to start him with reading, but he is nowhere near it."

"When will you assess him again?" I asked.

"I can assess him again in two weeks," she said. "In the meantime, we'll continue to work on letters and sounds."

"Thank you," I said, ending the call.

As soon as I hung up the phone, I burst into tears. I felt like someone had punched me in the gut, hard! Having a teacher tell me my child was not where he should be academically was difficult to hear for many reasons. First, I was a straight "A" student for most of my elementary, junior high, and high school career. Learning was fun and always came easy for me. Of course, I wanted the same for my child. Second, I spent a lot of time and energy motivating and encouraging my high school students to excel. How was my own child performing below the expected standard? Every night, my husband and I spent time working with him on writing, sight words, letters, and numbers. I thought we were doing a good job working to get him prepared for kindergarten. Did I forget to mention my son was four years old and in prekindergarten?

I was at work when I received the phone call. For the rest of the morning, I questioned whether I had done everything I needed to do to assist in my child's learning. Had I allowed him to watch too much television? Should I have put less emphasis on writing and more emphasis on letters and sounds? As an educator, shouldn't my son be the most prepared child in the class? I felt like a failure.

At the end of the day, my supervisor stopped by my room unexpectedly. I told him about the phone call and his response was refreshing. He simply told me not to rely on the assessment. He reminded me the assessment was subjective and could be influenced by many factors, including the patience of the assessor. He

145

advised me to assess my child and make a determination for myself. After speaking to my supervisor, I had a completely different perspective. When I met with my son's teacher later in the day, I was able to ask questions about the assessment with a clear mind.

If you are not aware of your own emotions and triggers, you can be easily distracted from your purpose, your goals, and your vision. One incident can completely throw you off in a way which disrupts the aspirations you have set for yourself. At the least, it can turn a good day into a bad day and make you less productive. At the most, it can prevent you from being as focused as you need to be on what is really important and keep you from fulfilling your destiny.

Relationships have always been an essential part of my life. I definitely value the people in my inner circle, including my close friends and family members. As a result, I have to be aware of how I allow conflict in my relationships to affect me. If you are the person your friends or family call when they have a problem, it is great to be a listening ear. Sometimes, the situation may call for you to lend your advice or a helping hand. However, you must be vigilant not to allow every emergency, crisis, or issue to become your personal crusade.

Unfortunately, there are people who have no intention to make their situation better. They will drain you of all your energy with their complaints, sad stories, and emergencies. By no means am I making light of the difficulties someone could be facing. However, if every time you speak to a person, she is telling you about a struggle, another obstacle, or a problem, you need to be aware of the purpose she serves in your life. If she never has good news or a story of overcoming to share, she may be depleting you of essential energy you need to put toward your goals. It will certainly be up to you to make the determination. Do not expect someone else to be vigilant on your behalf.

Being aware of how you use your time, talent, and energy does not require you to be suspicious of those around you. Most of the people around you are probably not operating out of malice. However, you can be asked to participate in positive, worthy causes which create a burden or strain. Shortly after getting married, my husband and I became highly involved in our church. While I had attended the church for two years prior to us marrying, we decided to join together once we were married. We both served in various capacities, but not usually on the same team at the same time. In addition to serving, I was also assisting one of the team leaders with a Bible study for the team. I was working full-time, writing my first book, and helping out whenever the church asked me. My first priority should have been to be a newlywed. While I enjoyed serving in the church, it did not take long for it to feel like an obligation. I found it difficult to refuse because it was the church. After a while, however, it became overwhelming.

One day, a good friend gave me much needed advice. He reminded me I was responsible for creating my schedule and filling my plate. No one else was going to tell me I had too much on my plate because it was mine. From the experience, I learned if people have a need and you can fill the need, they will have you fill it as long as you allow it. Do not expect anyone else to look out for your best interest. It is your responsibility to stay on guard.

Eventually, my husband and I were asked to assist in starting a new campus location for our church. My husband served as a lead usher and I was volunteering as a leader for the greeters. The new location was in a different area from where we lived and where the main campus was located. As a result, we were dealing with a different demographic, which included transients and homeless people. It was not uncommon for someone to enter the new campus location drunk or cause a disturbance during the service.

One Sunday morning, a woman seemingly intoxicated, entered the service and became belligerent when she was directed where she should sit. The campus pastor at the time instructed my husband to physically remove the woman from the premises. First, anyone who knows my husband knows he is very mild mannered and extremely respectful of women. It would be out of character for him to physically restrain or remove anyone. Second, he was not hired as security. He was volunteering his time as an usher. My husband adamantly refused to put his hands on the woman, which did not sit well with the campus pastor.

Although I was not usually an usher, I volunteered when needed. A couple of weeks after the incident, the campus pastor asked me to become the head usher, which would place me ahead of my husband, who had been serving in the position for months. I respectfully declined and we soon began attending services at the main campus, again. If I had not been aware of my responsibility to be a support to my husband, I might have taken the position. Although I doubt there was malice behind the campus pastor's request, at the very least it was reckless. He probably should have seen the potential for conflict in asking me to take a position which would usurp my husband. Fortunately, I saw it and knew better.

To stay focused on your goals and maintain your priorities, you must be vigilant about what you allow to take center stage in your thought life and your activities. Take time to gain the right perspective about every situation. Be careful not to become distracted by turning insignificant issues into major crises. Do not allow others to dictate how you manage your time and energy based on their needs. When your plate fills up, remember who filled it!

BE VIGILANT REFLECTION

❖ In what area of your life are your emotions likely to get the best of you? Why is it a sensitive area for you?

❖ Think of a situation in which you were not as vigilant as you should have been. What were the consequences? What did you learn from the experience?

❖ How can you be more vigilant regarding your time, talent, and energy? What are potential distractors for you?

BE WISE

"Knowing yourself is the beginning of all wisdom."
~Aristotle, Greek Philosopher

I have several scars on my arms and legs which are reminders of my various life experiences. I have a scar on my right arm which came from a childhood bruise. I got it while playing with some of my cousins. Although it is unsightly, it reminds me to always make time for fun. I also have a small scar from having a cesarean with my son, Tristan. I love that scar! It is a reminder of how some of the most painful experiences can bring about the greatest joy. Finally, I have two scars, each on a different leg, which are the results of two separate biopsies. I wear them with pride because they remind me to always make my health a priority.

I would not remove my scars because they each tell a story and represent a lesson I learned about myself. While you can certainly learn from the experiences of others, it is necessary to learn from your own experiences in life. The only way to become wise is to be willing to grow. Oprah Winfrey said, "Turn your wounds into wisdom." In my life, the two areas in which I have grown the most, and continue to grow, are in my finances and my relationships.

My great-grandmother always told me to save a nickel out of every dime. Oh how I wished I had listened! Her grandmother gave her the same advice. Although my great-grandparents were by no means wealthy, they always had enough. Somehow, I knew my great-grandmother was never completely without any money. At an early age, she took me to the bank and helped me open a savings account. As a teenager, I worked and learned how to budget my money by buying my own school clothes. When I finished college and began working full-time, I remembered the advice my great-grandmother gave me. Unfortunately, I did not apply it.

I was young, carefree, and living on my own. No husband. No children. Single in the city. I ate out almost every day of the week. Then, there was shopping. If I had a couple of hundred dollars left at the end of the month, I would put a little to the side for savings. However, the bulk of it went toward shopping. After acquiring quite a bit of credit card debt, I decided to handle my finances differently. Over time, I paid off the debt and started changing the way I managed money. I became more conscientious of my spending and saving. I would love to say I only had to learn the lesson once. Sometimes, however, it may take you a couple of times to get it right. Years later, I found myself in credit card debt, again. And, again, I had to evaluate my spending and saving habits. Today, as a work in progress, I am diligently trying not to repeat the same mistakes of my past.

Some people get into great financial trouble by looking at what their neighbors, co-workers or friends have and trying to compete. Comedian, Kevin Hart, warns "Stay in your financial lane!" Do not get caught up in what others have or what they are doing. With the popularity of social media, it is easy to access the lives of others and see what they have, what they are wearing, and where they are going. However, you may never know what they have to do in order to maintain the image. Quite frankly, you may not be willing to do what they have to do in order to live the lifestyle. Much of the time, they are only pretending to live the lifestyle you see.

I remember watching a popular reality television show about doctors. One couple had a luxurious mansion and the wife was a stay at home mother. In a later episode, the couple revealed they owed the IRS hundreds of thousands in back taxes, and the luxurious house in which they were living was rented. For the amount they were spending in rent, they could have easily purchased two fabulous homes. While they had made some financial missteps, I thought it was admirable of the couple to disclose and discuss their financial struggles on the show. They went through the process of having to downsize and shared how neither had come from a family making the amount of money to which they suddenly had access. Unfortunately, like many of us, they did not have a model or advisor to guide them in their financial decisions. Instead, they were learning from their mistakes. .

When it comes to money, you must know yourself. If you like electronics and gadgets, you know you will be tempted when the newest or latest tech craze comes out. Therefore, you should try to save for it during the lull between the last gadget and the next one to hit the market. Or, you should discipline yourself to only buy what you can afford at the time. If you love clothes and shoes, you might develop a strategy which allows you to enjoy retail therapy without going beyond your level of comfort.

In my case, I did not enjoy seeing clothes in my closet with price tags still on them knowing I would never wear them. Now, I typically only buy clothes when I need them or for a specific event. Doing so has helped me to avoid over shopping and regretting it later. Additionally, I discovered it gives me great joy to get a bargain. I do not want to pay more if paying less is an option.

Therefore, I look for coupon codes and discounts for shopping and traveling. Whether it is learning from your past experiences, seeking advice and resources, or developing your own money-saving or money-making strategies, it is important to know and understand what works best for you.

Much like we go through phases of financial growth, we also go through periods of growth in our relationships. The people in your life serve a purpose. Whatever the purpose, it is to help you develop into the person you are designed to be. While I have always been friendly, I have been selective about whom I have allowed into my inner circle. As a young adult, I believed the people whom I called friends would be my friends for life. When I began to experience the demise of some of my closest friendships, it was difficult to accept. Within a two year time period, I watched four of my closest relationships dissolve. It was during the year of my engagement and right after my marriage.

There was no betrayal or deception. There had not been a major argument or blowup. In each situation, the relationship gradually began to change. We no longer shared the same interests or values. We were in different places in our lives. The communication became less frequent and eventually, nonexistent. It was confusing and difficult for me to accept because I was experiencing a great feeling of euphoria in one area of my life, being newly married. However, I was saddened and grieving the loss of four relationships which were painfully significant to me.

Sometimes God needs to move people out of your life to make room for what he has planned. It does not mean you are good and they are bad. It just means the purpose has been served. It was a challenging concept for me to grasp because I initially felt rejected. When each of the relationships began to change, it took me longer to accept the change than it did for the other parties. They had already accepted they were traveling a different path or had decided they were not interested in maintaining the level of relationship we'd once shared. For me, however, the dissolution was abrupt and the finality was staggering.

It took me a couple of years to fully understand why it was necessary for those relationships to end. While they were all people whom I loved dearly, our purpose in one another's life was only for a season. When I reflected on each relationship, I saw how it was necessary for the period of time it thrived. However, I could also see qualities in each relationship which would not be conducive for where my life was heading.

Have you ever connected with a person while completing a project? The two of you may have bonded over a commonality or a goal on which you were both working. You may have even shared personal parts of your life while engaged in the project. However, when the project was over, you no longer had the same need or desire to meet with the person and share as you did when you were working together. It is a similar experience when people come into your life for a reason or season. They cannot stay because you are taking different roads and on a different timeline.

When I think about where my life is today, I understand why I am connected to the people currently in my life. My understanding is definitely a result of knowing who I am. When you know yourself and understand your purpose, you position yourself to understand the value other people bring into your life. If people are destined to be in your life for a lifetime, you grow and adapt together.

Being wise has less to do with intellect and much to do with your ability to process and learn from every experience in life. Boxing legend, Muhammad Ali, said "The man who views the world at fifty the same as he did at twenty has wasted thirty years of his life." If what you are doing does not serve a specific purpose, it is time to make a change. When you no longer give value to someone else or they no longer bring value to you, the season is over. Just remember, change is essential to growth. And, growth is essential for wisdom!

BE WISE REFLECTION

❖ Name the wisest person you know personally. Explain why you chose the person you selected.

❖ In what two areas have you experienced the most growth in the past year? Explain how you have grown in each area and the lessons you have learned from your experiences.

❖ If you could travel back in time ten years, what advice would you give your younger self? How can you apply the advice to your life today?

BE eXCELLENT

"When you live your life being excellent, you live a
life with no regrets."
~Asiah Wolfolk-Manning, Author and Speaker

*"You are not going to get straight A's on your report
card this term. You have a 93.4 in math. You need a 94
to get an A," Mr. Hicks said. He was my fifth grade
teacher and the devil, as far as I was concerned.*

*"What do you mean? I have a 93.4. Can't you give
me the tenth of the point?" I pleaded.*

*"No. I'm not going to give you the tenth of the point.
You need to learn you're not going to always be on top,"
he responded, coldly.*

*I sat in my fifth grade class and cried
uncontrollably. I had made straight A's on every report
card prior to having Mr. Hicks. He was going to give me
my first B and there was nothing I could do about it. My
classmates tried to console me by telling me it was okay,
while glaring at the teacher from hell. When I got home,
I cried even more about the worst day in my fifth grade
life.*

In the weeks after receiving the B, I worked harder
to ensure I made a clear A average in all my subjects. I
had survived what I had been dreading since I began
making straight A's – not being perfect. There was no
volcanic eruption. The world did not implode. My great-
grandparents were not disappointed in my efforts.
Instead, they were relieved to see me face a
disappointment, overcome it, and be okay. While I still do
not agree with Mr. Hick's reasoning, I am grateful for the
experience because I have learned several valuable
lessons from it.

No one is obligated to give you anything. At the time, I felt Mr. Hicks was being a jerk. However, he acted well within his right and discretion in giving me the B. Whatever you want in life, be prepared to work hard to get it and expect no handouts on the way. When you can do better, you must do better. I do not remember if the 93.4 B average was my best effort. However, the experience left the lasting impression to give my best effort each time.

The first year my law magnet students competed in the district mock trial competition was exciting. There were four rounds over two days. We knew we had won the first morning round. However, the first afternoon round was tough. Our team competed against a team of what seemed to be mini-lawyers. These high school kids walked and talked as if they'd already taken and passed the bar exam. While my students were no slouches, the opposing team was more polished and better prepared. The next day was about the same. We did well in the morning. However, during the afternoon round, our captains made a decision to substitute two team members with alternates who were less prepared. Needless to say, we lost the competition.

My students were disappointed because they were smart kids accustomed to winning. When I asked the team if they had given their best effort, they reluctantly admitted they had not. They had missed practices and did not prepare as much as they could have. For them, the loss was especially hurtful because they knew they were just as capable as the students who actually won the competition. Clearly, however, the students who defeated our team took the competition more seriously and gave excellent effort. Being smart is not always enough. Sometimes, it is the amount of effort you put forth which makes the difference.

I learned a similar lesson during my freshman year in college. I quickly discovered college algebra is nothing like high school algebra. The real struggle began my second semester in pre-calculus. Math had always been my least favorite subject. Early into the class, I was struggling to do well. I stayed after class for additional help and went to the professor during office hours. When I received my first C as a final grade, not surprisingly, it was in my college pre-calculus class. Unlike the fifth grader who needed the A to feel validated, I rejoiced in that C. It was a hard earned C, which I was proud to receive. I had done everything I could do and when it amounted to a C, it was good enough for me.

You do not have to be perfect to be exceptional. Additionally, winning or being at the top is not always a true reflection of excellence. You can give an outstanding effort and place third in the race. Although you will not take home the first place trophy, you can be proud of your performance knowing you did your best. As a child, I thought I needed to be perfect to be accepted. It may have been due to the absence of my parents and the need for approval. Whatever the reason, I embraced the idea of being a perfectionist as one of my strengths. Our strengths, however, are often our weaknesses to the extreme.

As a working attorney, if I had an upcoming trial, I spent my entire weekend reviewing case files and exhibits. Once the trial was over, I felt drained because I was out of balance. No one was pressuring me to be perfect, but I held myself to an unattainable standard. My expectation of perfection was not limited to my life.

Unfortunately, I often held those in my life to the same standard.

While we were engaged, my husband told me he was going to try a fast. Immediately, I responded by telling him what fasting was all about and how he needed to take it seriously. After I shared my infinite wisdom of having done one fast in my whole life, he was no longer interested. I had effectively discouraged him from even trying. As soon as I finished talking, I knew I had messed up. Who was I to tell him he wasn't ready to do whatever he felt God was calling him to do? I was way out of line and should have taken the time to listen rather than to speak. I had the perfect opportunity to be an excellent encourager. Instead, I had done an excellent job discouraging him with my need for perfection.

Rather than trying to lead a perfect life, strive to be a person of excellence. Allow the work you do to speak for you. When you make a commitment, you commit to give the best of yourself. This is true even when what you are doing is not exciting or does not feel rewarding. You will not always receive recognition or accolades for maintaining a standard of excellence. Yet, the situations in which you find it challenging to be a person of excellence are the times when it matters most.

Recently, I witnessed a patron in the library treat the young woman working behind the reference desk quite rudely. The desk clerk called out to the patron respectfully because another patron was waiting to enter a private study room. The rude patron became visibly angry and began yelling at the clerk in front of other patrons in the library. Rather than responding in a negative manner, the desk clerk kept her cool and said nothing. I watched as she waited on the next patron, smiling and greeting him courteously. Although she could have taken her frustration out on the next person, she seemingly let it roll right off of her. When it was finally my turn in line, I commended her for having such an outstanding attitude. I told her how admirable it was for her to maintain her composure in the presence of others, especially the youth in the library. What I had witnessed was someone choosing to be a person of excellence. In many situations, being excellent may require you to do what is unpopular and is often a demonstration of leadership.

The movie, *When the Game Stands Tall*, is about a high school football team in California with a record setting 151 game winning streak. The star running back, Chris Ryan, is slated to break the state's touchdown record during a tough championship game. In the final moments of the game, it is clear Ryan's team has won. When given the opportunity to score and break the state record, to everyone's surprise, Ryan takes a knee. He tells his teammates it would not be right to end his senior year with the team chasing after his personal victory. Instead, he honors the values his coach has taught him and finishes the game leading his team by example. It is a powerful lesson concerning character and excellence in leadership.

Whether you are working a job, doing volunteer work, or pursuing your passion, strive for excellence. It is not enough to do well when you know someone is looking or you are being evaluated. You should never become complacent with just being good. Author Jim Collins said, "Good is the enemy of great." As long as you are okay with being good, you will never work to achieve greatness. Make excellence a standard because the way you practice is the way you play.

BE eXCELLENT REFLECTION

❖ What does it mean to live a life of excellence? In what area in your life could you strive to be more excellent?

❖ Name three people you consider to be excellent people. Explain why you chose the people you selected. What characteristics make them excellent?

❖ Think about a time when you gave less than an excellent effort. What was the reason? What did you learn from the experience?

BE YOURSELF

"In a world where you can be anything, be yourself."
~Etta Turner, Slain Rotary International Exchange
Student

I heard a story about a gardener who had two pots he used to water plants. One of the pots was perfectly molded and could hold a full portion with no problem. The other pot had a crack on the side which allowed water to run out. Each day, the gardener traveled to the stream to fill the two pots with water. On his way back home, he noticed water running out of the pot with the crack in it. By the time he returned home, the pot without the crack was completely full. However, the cracked pot only had half of the water he'd originally placed in it. The gardener made the same journey to and from the stream for months.

One day, as the gardener arrived back to his home, the cracked pot said to him, "Oh, how I wish I was like the perfect pot! The perfect pot can hold all its water. But, I can only give you half." The gardener responded, "Why would you say a thing like that? Aren't you aware of the good work you have done? Just look at the beautiful flowers along the road. Each day, you water them as we travel back from the stream. Sure, the perfect pot supplies more water for my plants. But, you help flowers grow for anyone traveling along the road to see."

The cracked pot was surprised. While he was busy wanting to be like the perfectly molded pot, he had failed to recognize his own significance.

The world is beautiful and filled with variety because you are different from everyone else. Every individual has a unique set of talents, skills, and gifts.

164

Although you may share common interests, there are no two people who share the same talents, thoughts, beliefs, or personality. You are an original and can never be replicated.

Unfortunately, many people spend their lives trying to be something or someone other than who they are. In some cases, people go to extreme measures, even placing their health and life in jeopardy. On a television show about plastic surgery, the woman on the show had previously undergone several surgeries on her face, breasts, and butt which left her looking disfigured. She had even allowed someone without a medical license to inject cement into her face and butt.

It was difficult to watch and not wonder why someone would go to such extremes to change her appearance. The doctors on the show assumed the challenge of correcting the botched surgeries and when they were finished, the woman looked better than she did prior to the doctors' help. However, the damage was done. She would never look like her original self.

You should be happy and feel confident when you look in the mirror. I am not suggesting there is anything wrong with wanting to improve how you look if it is going to make you feel better about yourself. I wear makeup to enhance my beauty, but I feel just as good without makeup as I do with it. I exercise to stay healthy and fit, in part, because I want to feel good about what I see in the mirror. However, I know my value is not determined by the size I am wearing.

If given the option, most people would like to change something about themselves. Maybe you are short and would like to be tall. Perhaps you have always been thin and would like to have curves. All over the world, people make alterations to their physical appearance to conform to society's definition of beauty. If society says thin is in, people take diet pills and engage in unhealthy weight loss practices to look like someone on a magazine cover. If society says curves are beautiful, people start getting injections and implants to plump up. If you allow society to dictate what is beautiful, you will find yourself in a constant struggle to meet the demands and expectations of an unattainable standard.

If you are trying to look like the images you see in celebrity photos, you are setting yourself up for failure. During an interview, 90s supermodel, Cindy Crawford, ironically admitted to wishing she looked like "Cindy Crawford" when she woke up in the morning. In essence, she was saying what you see on the magazine cover is an illusion created by a production team, including hair, makeup, stylists, lighting, and Photoshop.

To get the perfect picture, models are tweaked and pulled in different directions. Fans are used to create wind for blowing hair. Photoshop is used to erase moles, freckles, and blemishes which exist in real life, but will never make it on the magazine cover. Curves and muscles are added to enhance the body, or deleted depending on what is trendy. Then, real women purchase the magazines and aspire to achieve an imaginary level of perfection. Find true beauty in being yourself. If you have moles and rolls, whether you embrace them or erase them, you are still who you are.

People who are fair-skinned want to be darker so they lay in the sun and go to tanning salons, at the risk of getting cancer. Likewise, many people with dark skin want to be lighter so they use toxic bleaching creams to lighten their skin. When I was young, I did not appreciate my big legs and full lips. Now, it tickles me to know people actually spend money to make their lips look like mine. I never would have guessed people have surgery to get the kind of calves I have naturally. One of the greatest gifts you can give yourself is self-acceptance. Beauty based trends fluctuate from year to year. You will stay in an up and down shift if your confidence level and acceptance of yourself is dependent upon the world's acceptance of you.

When I get dressed or go shopping, I do not need to ask anyone's opinion about how an outfit looks. As long as I like it, it looks good! I am not waiting around for someone to validate me. My husband often compliments me and tells me I look nice. While I enjoy receiving compliments from my husband, my level of confidence is not dependent upon what he says or thinks.

Knowing who you are and loving who you are is a great sense of empowerment. When you see other people excelling in an area in which they are skilled or gifted, you should not feel envious or even wish you could do what they are doing. You have your own unique set of gifts and talents. You should not want to change the characteristics which make you unique to conform and be like anyone else. Your unique characteristic, quality, talent, or feature is what sets you apart.

Naturally, I have a very high pitched voice. Whenever I am angry or excited, it becomes even higher. Without meaning to be hurtful, a close friend once told me my voice was annoying. Ouch! As a speaker, I could have allowed myself to become self-conscious about my voice. If I had focused on what my friend said, self-doubt may have kept me from moving forward as a speaker. Instead, I remembered what Joyce Meyer said about her voice. She has a deep voice and has often been mistaken for being a man over the phone. However, God has used her voice to reach and teach millions of people.

Because her voice is so distinct, no one ever confuses her with any other speaker. Her voice is her gift! Much like Joyce Meyer, I believe my unique voice will be instrumental in me fulfilling my purpose.

If you do not know who you are, get to know yourself. Embrace your likes, dislikes, talents, gifts, and areas which need improving. I like laughing with friends, but I am comfortable being by myself. Exercise and healthy living are important to me, but I love food. I enjoy watching crime dramas like *Dateline* and *48 Hours Mystery*, but I also enjoy classic sitcoms such as, *The Golden Girls* and *Friends*. I can be loud at times and will aggressively defend my position, hence my decision to become a lawyer. In contrast, I can be overly sensitive. Although I am a work in progress, I am not trying to be anyone other than who I am because I like myself.

I once heard a story about a girl named Amy, who wanted to be like Erica. She thought Erica was the coolest girl in school. So, she attempted to walk and talk like Erica. She even imitated the way Erica dressed. Meanwhile, Erica looked up to Jennifer and thought if she could just be more like Jennifer, she would have it made. Erica began to imitate everything Jennifer did. Unbeknownst to Erica, Jennifer admired Charity because everyone seemed to like Charity. As a result, Jennifer watched Charity and mimicked Charity's style. What no one knew was Charity had always been impressed with Amy's self-confidence. Therefore, she tried to emulate everything Amy did, including her walk, her talk, and her personality. In the end, Amy was really just following a different version of herself.

As Ralph Waldo Emerson said in his essay, *Self-Reliance*, there comes a time in every man's life when he realizes "…envy is ignorance and imitation is suicide." Be the person God made you to be. You will always be a better you than anyone else!

BE YOURSELF REFLECTION

❖ Think of a time when you wanted to be like someone else or did not adequately represent your true character. What did you learn from the experience?

❖ What is one quality or characteristic which makes you unique or different? How do you embrace the quality or characteristic?

❖ What are three character traits you love about yourself? How do the traits show up in your life?

BE ZEALOUS

"You've gotta dance like there's nobody watching,
Love like you'll never be hurt,
Sing like there's nobody listening,
And live like it's heaven on earth."
~William W. Purkey, Author and Educational Leader

After writing my first book, I decided to attend the Miami International Book Fair as a vendor. Tens of thousands of people from all over the world attend the fair each year. As a new author, I thought it would be great exposure for my book. For several weeks leading up to the fair, I worked on making promotional materials. During the week of the fair, I pulled all-nighters getting everything prepared. The fair was a three day event, and though I had little sleep, I was present each day to promote my new book. By the end of the fair, I think I had only sold five books.

My great-grandmother, who is usually very supportive, attended the event with me. I can still remember her disappointment with the book sales. As we packed up to leave on the last day, I recall her saying, "Five books. That's all we sold in three days!" She was in disbelief, but I was unmoved. While I wanted to sell books, I was not discouraged by the outcome. Writing is my passion and part of my purpose. Attending the book fair was simply one of many events to come. I chose to view the experience as a learning opportunity rather than a disappointment.

Although my grandmother was not trying to be negative, her comments could have had a negative effect. I could have joined in with her and looked at the event as a failure. It could have been easy to view it as a waste of time, energy, and money. However, you have to learn in order to grow and move closer to achieving your ultimate goal. As a result, it is important to surround yourself with positive people who are like-minded. Do not hesitate to stop those around you from making comments or statements which have negative connotations.

Once I explained I was not disappointed, my grandmother began to encourage me, which was helpful. When you are zealous about what you do, your enthusiasm should not be easily deflated. Rather than focusing on what did not happen, I chose to focus on what I needed to do in the future. I have not yet returned to the Miami International Book Fair, but I will. When I attend the next time, I will be an invited author and my book sales will certainly be more than five.

What energizes you? For what are you willing to stay up all night and work? What are you willing to do for free? When you have passion for what you do, you are willing to put your all into it. I have given hundreds of presentations, but each time I take the stage I get butterflies in my stomach. Before speaking, I feel a mixture of nervous energy and excitement. The butterflies are not from fear, but rather from the passion I have for speaking. Each time I have the opportunity to use my gift, I am so energized. I can hardly contain my enthusiasm.

As a teacher, it is great to hear students express a passion or love for something. In my experience, when students have a passion for what they study, they generally do well in the area. I have found this to be especially true with athletes, particularly football players. The male students I teach who play football talk about the game whenever they are given the chance. Anytime they can make a correlation to football or use an example from the game to express their point, they do. While I encourage all my students to be well-rounded and gain exposure from the world around them, the passion most football players exhibit is undeniable. Whether it is in freezing weather or sweltering heat, the players get out on the field and play the game they love. Isn't that what passion is all about? When you have a passion, you will pursue it despite the weather report. You will do it even if others laugh at you. You will find energy to work on it while everyone else is sleeping.

Have you ever seen the commercials which are a compilation of greatest Olympics moments or surprising victories? There might be a clip of a track star who fell behind and worked her way back to place first. You might see a swimmer who was the underdog and surprised everyone by finishing on top. Or, maybe it is a gymnast whose stumble could have left her feeling defeated, but she continued like a champion. I often become emotional when I see those commercials because I understand the passion it takes to make it to the level of the Olympics. It takes great determination and discipline to pursue such a dream. When I see someone crying because they are victorious, I empathize. Even though I do not know him personally, I know he had to have passion. I recognize his drive and his work ethic. Like most champions, I know his success story was not overnight.

If someone asked you for what are you willing to die, the most common answer would likely be family, or maybe even respect. However, a better question is – For what are you willing to *live*? Without passion and purpose, one does not live but merely exist. If you have not discovered a cause, a belief, a talent, or a gift which moves you to think outside of yourself, you are missing out on living life with passion.

I have discovered my purpose in life is to empower, inspire, and impact the world through words. Years ago, I realized I am not only passionate about writing and speaking, but I have a gift for it. I am not being arrogant, as I rarely can even remember what I have written after the words make it to the paper. That's how I know it is a gift! It is larger than me and my ability. Most certainly, God has equipped me with this skill. While I continue to take classes and workshops to improve, I know my ability to reach others through my words is a spiritual gift. The reason I have been able to pursue my purpose while working a full-time job is because I am zealous about it. My passion fuels my purpose.

There have been nights when I worked for hours practicing my speech for an upcoming engagement. Many times, I am the last to leave the library or coffee house while working on a writing project. The irony is I am usually exhausted from working a full day at my job, but also energized because my passion is what I love. When you have passion for what you do, it shows through your attitude and your results.

While it is important to know your purpose in life and pursue it, you should be passionate about life in general. Learn to see the beauty in the world around you and live a life of expectancy. Get excited about the day and what is yet to come. Life can be pretty routine and mundane if you allow it to be. You wake up, go to work, come home, and repeat. However, there is a whole lot going on inside of twenty-four hours and much of it has to do with your perspective. If you are bored with your life, you are not living with passion. Take up a new hobby, learn a different language, or start a home project. Find a cause for which you are willing to advocate by giving your time, money, or talent. With the right attitude,

174

you can even be motivated by everyday tasks like playing with your dog.

Although I never had a pet growing up and was always afraid of dogs, my husband grew up differently. He comes from a dog-loving family and always had a dog as a pet. Reluctantly, I agreed to get one under the condition the dog was very small. When we first bought our little Yorkie, Coco, I was a novice. Six years later, I have learned a few valuable lessons. Coco has mastered the art of living enthusiastically. While he thoroughly enjoys playing fetch with a squeaky toy, he can turn something as ordinary as my sock into an adventure. Even though he is only eight pounds, you would never know it. Whether it is someone passing by the door or another dog sniffing around, Coco's bark rivals that of a German Shephard. Perhaps, however, Coco's zeal for life is best demonstrated by the way he greets us each day. No matter how many times he has seen me, my husband, or Tristan walk through the front door, he wags his tail incessantly as if it is our first meeting. Wouldn't it be great if more people responded to life in such a way?

Living a zealous life has much to do with your attitude and mindset. When you discover what matters most to you in life, you want to put your energy into it. Focus on the gifts and talents you have been given and put them to good use. Think about what you have to offer the world. Last but not least, consider what you enjoy doing. If you are reading this book, it means you still have breath in your body. As long as there is breath, there is life. You were meant to live your life with passion and not simply exist. Make a conscious decision to live a zealous life and give your existence meaning!

BE ZEALOUS REFLECTION

❖ Explain the difference between living life and merely existing. Where do you fall on the spectrum of living and existing?

❖ Describe how you can live life with more zeal. What changes would you need to make? What resources would you need?

❖ Think about your purpose in life. Why are you here? What steps can you take to fully become who you were created to be?